the roughneck or the poet?

American women telling the raw naked truth

ALEC GENTRY

Copyright © 2013 Alec Gentry & Stephen Howard
www.roughneckpoet.com

All rights reserved.
No part of this book may be reproduced or transmitted in any form or by any means, graphic, electronic or mechanical, including photocopying, recording or by any information storage and retrieval system without the written permission of the author/publisher, except for the inclusion of brief quotations in a review.

ISBN: 978-0-9895448-0-1

particular house

PICTURES, EDITING & BOOK DESIGN by STEPHEN HOWARD

author's note

The remarks quoted and the stories related in this book are drawn from real people and events. Certain names, places, occupations, and other identifying details have been changed where necessary. Some individuals and circumstances are composites.

To my clients, mentors and friends who wanted to see this collection in print. This book belongs to all the women who shared their deepest and darkest with me, who trusted me with their truth laid bare. I'm grateful to every one.

contents

	acknowledgements	ix
	initiation	p 1
1	truth serum	p 7
2	what about us?	p 11
3	at war with each other	p 21
4	behind every man..?	p 29
5	the war against men	p 39
6	psychotherapy	p 55
7	sex	p 63
8	a fuck-buddy is...	p 75
9	damaged goods	p 81
10	penis size	p 91
11	man-haters	p 99
12	lies	p 109

13	jealousy	p 117
14	out of my league	p 127
15	relationships & marriage	p 137
16	feminism	p 147
17	children & parenting	p 155
18	mothers	p 165
19	abuse & control	p 173
20	regrets	p 183
21	the internet	p 193
22	a man's view	p 201
23	married & loving it	p 221
	aftershock	p 227

acknowledgements

Patsy Billings, a.k.a. *Ms. B.*

Thank you for your patience. Thank you for sharing your wisdom. Thank you for defending me on the few occasions when I was right about State Board Rules & Regulations. You are the most elegant gentlewoman I've ever met, and knowing you inspired me to raise my bar. That's probably why I'm still single—again.

Dr. Karin Kappen

Thank you for making a simple roughneck believe he could be a writer, even though he may have seemed "a little awkward" at times. You've made a lasting difference.

Patricia Preston

In loving memory of my finest mentor.

initiation

roughneck [ˈruhf-nek] noun

1. a rough, coarse person; tough.
2. any laborer working on an oil-drilling rig.

    I was born a third-generation oilfield worker. At sixteen years old I dropped out of high school to become a roughneck on an oil-drilling rig. Before I knew it I was making more money than most adult men with college degrees. My earnings attracted a beautiful young girl who hated her mother and needed a place to live. A week into our six-month relationship, she told me "Except for one time, I'm a virgin." "Cool," I said—"What's a virgin?"

    Settling down wasn't the first thing on my 16-year-old mind, but when that sweet girl tucked her hands into the back pockets of her 501's, tilted her head a little, and drilled holes through me with her big brown eyes, I turned to shit. Like a game warden with a tranquilizer dart, she tagged me and made me her own.

    Six years later on a cold rainy morning, the drilling-rig floor I was working on collapsed and I broke my back. After eighteen months of scrawny disability payments and fighting with Workers'

Compensation, my doctor finally released me. When I reported back to work I was told that injured workers were never rehired.

I was sent to a rehabilitation counselor to retrain me for a different occupation. For six long weeks a woman with a college degree studied me, tested me, and made her decision about my future. When she finally invited me to her office to reveal my new career, I was excited. I had imagined becoming an attorney, a doctor, or even an astronaut. "I have good news" she said, as if I'd won the lottery. When she told me I'd be working at a local hardware store for one-fourth my previous wages, I was shocked. The future astronaut that had walked into that office was now one very pissed-off roughneck! I came up out of my chair, planted my palms on her desk, and scowled.

When it became clear that her offer was taken as an insult, she said my only other option was to enroll in a vocational school to learn a trade. Okay, I was interested. Then she informed me that the only vocational school in my area was a beauty college. The room went quiet. She stared at me, waiting. I stared back. I was certain that she was certain a roughneck like me would choose a cut in pay over a career in hairstyling. I had been set up! The endless staring continued. And then, "Sign me up!" Of the two of us, I couldn't say who was more surprised.

Three weeks later I was standing in front of a beauty college with a duffle bag full of scissors, curlers, and hairpins. Now, I happen to really like girls, but being surrounded by a hundred of them at once was kind of scary. I was relieved when another male student arrived, until he asked the girls if he could borrow their mascara and eyeliner. I had to remind myself that I'd still receive my disability checks until I could find a real job. But six weeks into my Cosmetology course another voice in my head nagged "Alec, you can *do* this!"

After just one year I opened my first salon offering perms, cuts, and nails. I made a killing. But what I didn't count on was how much I would learn about the opposite sex. For nearly the next thirty years, and for some reason unknown to me, my clients welcomed me into the secretive and mysterious world of women. I had to tell my Dad that he was wrong, wrong about girls—they are *not* dumb.

My first year in business showed me how interested these women were to know just what other women were thinking, saying, and doing. Without using names, I would mention to one client something about another, and they *loved* it! Soon, I couldn't help wondering if they were coming to me for a great haircut or for the latest dirt. By the end of my second year I had received more than a hundred requests—no, demands—that I write a book about what women are *really* like. The idea spread like wildfire, and women couldn't wait to contribute. There were some disputes, but the one thing all my clients agreed upon is that American women are at odds with American men, and it's not a good thing. The traditional virtues that once gave women power and influence, and earned the respect of men and women alike, have all but disappeared from our culture. For almost thirty years my clients shocked me speechless, made me laugh uncontrollably and, on occasion, even made this crusty old roughneck cry.

My education continued, and a consistent profile of the average American woman emerged. Nearly all my clients wondered "How many of us are like this?" Years of polling and compiling statistics revealed a firm consensus of opinion. Thousands of women agreed that, to one degree or another, roughly 85% of American women reflect the thoughts, beliefs, and behaviors contained in these pages. A lot of these conversations had to do with "the war against men." I was continually reminded that even women who are not currently engaged in the battle retain the ability, at a moment's notice, to rally their dormant skills and rejoin the fight. Perhaps more telling is that most of these women compete in battle against each other in even more calculating and vicious ways. Does this mean that only 15% of heterosexual American women are able or willing to contribute responsibly to their personal relationships or to polite society? As the statistics were made known to the very clients who had shaped them, the card-carrying 85% issued a warning to the minority: "Keep a close eye on your men *or we'll eat them alive*." Members of this minority speak their mind in chapter 23.

The quotes in this book are taken from thousands of hour-long, one-on-one conversations. My fear of inaccurately representing these women was put to rest each time a new client joined the dialogue, and I heard once again "You know *way* too much about women!" The opinions and beliefs expressed in these quotes are not mine. They belong to the actual authors who agreed that, for thirty years, they revealed to me what women don't often share with a man—the truth.

From the start, the value and credibility of this effort have been challenged time and time again. On the phone years after we separated, my once-young girlfriend accused me of "just quoting a bunch of whores in a beauty shop." So I asked her "Don't you go to a beauty shop?" "Fuck you!" she explained, and hung up on me. Among other challenges, some have argued that these stories and confessions were just the opinions of women in my area. I'll let the record speak for itself. My clients' ages varied from eight years to ninety-one years old, and each and every one of them had a story to tell. I've been a licensed cosmetologist in California, Washington, Arizona, and Virginia. I've worked in twenty-six different salons in the U.S. and Mexico. I was employed as a cosmetology instructor at four different beauty colleges where I taught up to 160 students at a time. It was my privilege to serve women from seventeen different countries, and from every one of the United States. Interestingly, my foreign clients seemed most willing to comment. Apparently the behavior of American women is talked about worldwide.

When I've shared these stories with women who were never clients of mine, I was accused of being a misogynist. What the hell was a misogynist? After looking it up in the dictionary, I was shocked—"That's just not true!" I adore women. My mother and my two sisters happen to be women, and I love them dearly. Women are the most powerful, fascinating, and persuasive beings on the planet. They can start wars, make men write bad checks, break hearts into millions of pieces and, in their spare time, inspire breathtaking masterpieces. I mean, really—women talked me into writing this goddamn book, didn't they? And just for the record, I *hate* writing, and I'm still confused about the virginity thing.

Alec G.
roughneck hairstylist

1 truth serum

I was at a loss. If women were so determined to keep men in the dark, why were they so open and honest with me? I didn't have long to wait for the answer, and I never even got around to asking the question.

In my first year of business a well-known pastor's wife brought her daughter in for a haircut. As I started working on the girl's hair, her mother commenced *unloading!* She told me about her husband's duties as pastor, which included counseling parishioners for their Christian weaknesses. By the time I finished the haircut, the pastor's wife had delivered up a hair-raising earful of the congregation's scandalous deeds, complete with names (many of whom were my clients) and she described each sinful act in living color. She paid for the haircut, thanked me, and left my salon. Slightly traumatized by her stories, I hoped I could behave naturally the next time I saw the people she had named.

The phone rang less than fifteen minutes later. She was mortified by what she'd done, and she begged me to never speak of what she had told me. I gave her my word as a hairstylist and assured her that my reputation, as well, depended on my integrity. She tried to explain what compelled her to break every rule in the book—to gossip about things her husband shouldn't even have shared with her. As she groped for words I reassured her that there was no need for concern, but she persisted. "I just felt comfortable, I guess. Maybe it's the atmosphere of your salon. My god, it's like truth serum—I couldn't shut up!"

When a new client sat in my chair there was no way to know how soon she'd begin to unpack her personal details. Some clients studied me for months before sharing their secrets, while others thunderstruck me on the first visit. Nancy was a new nail client and ten minutes into her first appointment she asked "So, Alec—what do you think about anal sex?" She was a beautiful and petite 25-year-old personal secretary who was dating a rising young trial lawyer. A few months into their relationship, he suggested anal sex to "turn up the heat" in the bedroom. Nancy was appalled, but she worried that her unwillingness to allow him this activity might end their relationship. I'd been appointed mediator without my consent and, as I recall, I responded with something like "Uhhhhh—well, you know..." and "Okay, let's think about this—hmmmm..." This led to a very confused young woman, and an old guy with a foot in his mouth. The upside was that she loved her nails and, thankfully, never addressed the topic again.

I still can't explain this phenomenon, but day after day my clients were willing to offer up the deepest and often darkest secrets of their lives, and repeatedly insisted that I compile them into a book. More than a few have commented on this effect. What follows is a sampling.

"I can't believe I blab my brains out every time I see you. I think it's because you're touching me—that's got to be it."
Donna J. 49
newspaper editor

"You're like a bartender, huh? You probably hear *everybody's* problems."
Macy T. 31
factory worker

"Am I the only one who tells you everything?—*No?* Oh my god, how do you sleep at night?"
Trisha R. 33
home healthcare

"You're not recording this, are you? If you are, I'll have to kill you—and then myself."
Keela S. 44
elementary schoolteacher

"You know what's weird?—I tell *you* the truth and you haven't even asked for it. Normally, I lie."
Mercy D. 24
dental hygienist

"I want to know what people think about what I've done, but I don't want anyone to know it was me that did it."
Christa G. 32
clothing store manager

2 what about us?

"Women are completely fucked-up! I know because I am one."
    Theresa K. 47
    bartender

"Sure we fuck everything up, but we won't admit it. Even if we get caught in the act it's still somebody else's fault."
    Rose G. 41
    retail clerk

"You know what I don't get?—why is being vulgar so popular? What in the hell has happened to us?"
    Margo V. 46
    title officer

"A lot of women would trade their careers for a good man to take care of them. The problem is, if they find one they don't know what the hell to do with him. They don't feel they deserve a good man, and they're probably right!"
    Tara M. 29
    personal secretary

"Misery and melodrama are in vogue. If we aren't miserable, we don't have friends."
    Kayla A. 22
    college student

"The difference between our grandmothers and us is that our grandmothers developed their own personality. Today we use the media or friends to tell us how to be. My grandma was a real self-made woman. She was elegant."
Gabby H. 40
insurance agent

"We're just a big flock of sheep, always looking for someone to tell us how to look and how to think. The only difference between us and sheep is, the sheep aren't predators."
Misty L. 53
unemployed

"Women will buy *anything*. Look at TV commercials—they use cartoons and stupid people to get us to buy shit we don't need, and it works. Wow!—now I feel *really* stupid!"
Dana S. 39
school bus driver

"Have you listened to women lately? When the fuck did they start talking baby talk through their nose? Is it insecurity?—or immaturity?"
Sandy R. 43
restaurant manager

"I hate working with women—I'd rather work with men. There is nothing more miserable than an office full of women. They're backstabbers."
Cathy R. 44
collections agent

"We sell them on becoming doctors, lawyers, or some company bigshot—it's bullshit! Most women don't have the motivation or the money to succeed. That's why college is just a manhunt for most of them. The problem is, if a man marries a woman who has dropped out of college and failed herself, he's screwed."
Barbara S. 54
college counselor

"So many women are 'wannabees' and 'gonnabees'. They talk about what they wanna be and what they're gonna be in order to compensate for their perceived failings, but they don't follow up. After multiple failures with men, they equate success with a life that

doesn't include a man. They make big plans for college or opening a business, but then they meet another man and it's all over."
Noreen E. 46
therapist

"We're so fucked-up, the kind of man we want changes every day. Depending on what TV show or romantic movie we watch, it can change just like that—*Poof!* If I feel fat, I'm attracted to losers. If I lose fifteen pounds I want a babe. It makes it hard to stay in one relationship, like the one I'm in right now."
Cassie B. 37
grocery clerk

"Who doesn't want to be like the beautiful women on TV? But do you realize how much work that would be? We want the cool stuff, but we're lazy and fat, and I love ice cream."
Jennifer C. 28
photo processor

"We call ourselves 'bitches' like we're proud of it. We have T-shirts and bumper stickers calling ourselves bitches. And we gripe about the men we attract?—*Holy fuck!*"
Tina H. 40
interior decorator

"We don't want a man for love—he's a paycheck."
Renee B. 54
hardware store clerk

"American women must have their own job, house, and car. They spend too much for nothing. Their parents still pay their bills. My family works together and we need nothing. We travel, we drive new cars, and we take care of each other. Our children are never babysat or out-of-control."
Jihye K. 29
self-employed

"Women used to be attracted to the masculine breadwinner type. Now the weak and feminine guys get the girls. My daughter has one, and he doesn't have a job so she pays his way. I try to talk to her, but she just gets mad."
Carla P. 39
real estate agent

"Women are acting like teenagers! Older women are so immature and loose it embarrasses me. I'm afraid for my boyfriend because they hit on him and he likes it!"
Tami R. 20
college student

"There's only one word to describe women—spoiled rotten."
Debbie C. 24
makeup artist

"We're all in denial. The thing about denial is that you don't know you're in it. It's like being an asshole—everyone knows but you."
Molly L. 33
certified teen counselor

"Women have become so uneducated, they speak in clichés: *'It is what it is—Let's just agree to disagree—Whatever—You wouldn't understand, it's a girl thing'*. It must be a relief to not have to think."
Karen E. 56
high-school teacher

"We think we're better than men because we can 'multi-task.' Multitasking just means less quality. We buy into this crap to try to feel better than some man. Why do we need to feel better?"
Veronica Q. 46
housewife/mother

"We have given up our virtue. To be virtuous doesn't mean abstinence from sex, it means knowing the value of it. High-school girls are having anal sex with multiple partners and bragging about it. Can you imagine what that's doing to their future?"
Nancy W. 48
health department nurse

"All my friends say that being a bitch is the way to survive. My friends are all single and they drink way too much. I don't think being a bitch is a good thing."
Rhonda D. 24
dental receptionist/student

"I'd hate to be a man in this world. Women are all addicted to melodrama and money, and we can't manage either one."
Julie N. 33
hairstylist

"We can be smart if we want, but why bother? Dumb girls get all the attention."
Dianna P. 17
student

"Low self-esteem is bullshit! Self-esteem is what happens when you do something you're proud of. Low self-esteem isn't like acne or split-ends, it's lack of accomplishment. Everybody's a shade-tree psychiatrist diagnosing each other with low self-esteem because they've screwed up their life. How can you eat yourself into oblivion, fuck a bunch of men, have bastard children with a bunch of different guys and claim to have low self-esteem?—*Puh-leeze!* It makes me sick that we've become so damn lazy!"
Alice W. 57
Girl Scout leader/mother of 6

"I'm sorry to say, but American women are so lazy. American women could have everything in a prouder way."
Jasia V. 31
registered dietician

"Nature gave us different chores from men. We have a hymen, a uterus, and breasts. What about this is a man's fault? We should be the glue that holds society together. We have the ability to make a good man better than he knew he could be. We're not fighting with men, we're fighting with Mother Nature."
Janice T. 35
daycare owner

"Women's behavior is totally self-destructive. They act like they won't live past thirty. They like being party animals and bragging about all the sex they have. A nightclub and a strange bed won't prepare you for life."
Holly J. 41
casino dealer

"Women ridicule men when they say 'It's a man thing,' like they're all idiots. Men are different from women and that's the way it should be. It's a woman's job to find a man good enough and ready enough to be her children's father. Degrading men hurts us more than it does the men."
Elisa U. 61
housekeeping service owner

"We're mean and cruel. Not just to men, but to other women too. Hey, we want what we want and we do what we have to, to get it."
   Bethany F. 23
   motel housekeeper

"Women are sick screwed-up bitches! They get their big wedding, show off for their friends, and when the damn honeymoon's over they get all frigid. Sex is how they got him in the first place, and then they cut him off!—how stupid is that? Women would have a lot more money if they kept their marriage vows—like love and cherish."
   Mikki O. 26
   escort/exotic dancer

"I work with so many unmarried women who pretend they're independent. The truth is, they have a large group of family and bed partners to cover their bills. They've actually told me they hate independence, but they don't know how to escape it."
   Francine D. 64
   corporate administrator

"We women are so gullible we'll believe anything without checking to see if it's true. That's why so few women are experts on anything except what others have said or done before them."
   Hilda M. 52
   philosophy professor

"I hate being a woman. We're expected to be mean, so I *am* mean. I feel threatened by other women if I act happy and nice. They'll eat me alive."
   Hillary G. 41
   retail clerk

"If you're not miserable, you don't fit in at work. Everybody will call you stuck-up and make fun of you. I'm really happy with my life, so I make stuff up to gripe about at work."
   Mandi E. 27
   food server

"We have a tabloid mentality. We read it or hear about it, and then we're experts. Pretty sad, huh?"
   Teresa T. 29
   fast-food worker

"We're just working robots. I'm more loyal to my job than to my husband and kids. Work has everything I need—money, people to complain with, and I can even get laid if I want!"
Kindra B. 25
office worker

"We get so bored without melodrama. Work is boring, marriage is boring, paying bills is boring—so we create melodrama. My husband should be grateful because if he didn't let me screw with his mind, I would've been gone a long time ago. Do women share with each other?—*Absolutely!* We get together at work and bash the hell out of our men. It's entertainment."
Mary S. 34
retail sales

"My grandma said we all act this way because we're waiting for the other shoe to drop. I still don't know what the hell that means."
Kim Y. 19
receptionist

"When American women travel, they leave their morals at home. They say 'What happens here, stays here.' We keep them away from our men. They don't have education and they only speak one language. American women are the hillbillies of the international stage."
Catalina H. 35
language professor

"When I interview a new hire, her cleavage is the first thing I look at. If she comes to work showing too much cleavage, she'll spend more time managing her blouse than she will working. And she'll be more interested in who's looking at her tits than she is about customer service. I've had a few employees that were obsessed with their own tits, and I wouldn't hire another one."
Nadine C. 54
business owner

"If you really think about it, we've lost our minds! I wish my parents had picked a husband for me—*Naw,* that wouldn't work. I would have fought it."
Tawny C. 31
telemarketing

THE ROUGHNECK *or* THE POET?

"Women don't forget *anything*. We remember birthdays, anniversaries, and everyone we ever slept with in great detail. We can hold a grudge for life. The biggest lie I could tell you is 'I don't remember.'"
Letty Q. 27
tollbooth attendant

"All women are snoops. When you're in the shower, we'll go through your wallet, your desk, your closet, and especially the pictures on your computer. In a few minutes we'll have a profile on you that would make the FBI envious."
Darlene M. 33
medical receptionist

"Women used to think they had a way out if they burned all their bridges. They thought that if they got fat or ruined their reputation, they could fuck an older guy to get a car and a house. Things have changed and women are out of options now, because a 50-year-old man can buy two drinks and have his way with any 21-year-old girl in the bar. We've already lost the goddamn war against men and we don't even know it."
Robyn W. 44
office manager

"A smart girl never pays for drinks or a boob job—that's what men are for. My boobs cost my ex-boyfriend $8,500. You wanna see them?"
Chrissy D. 28
thrift store clerk

"Have you heard that human beings only use ten percent of their brains? Well, guess what?—women have cut that in half. We're economizing!"
Barbara T. 45
x-ray technician

"A woman isn't even capable of the same kind of love as a man. Men can go insane with love for a woman, and I'm jealous. I had a man fall in love with me like that once, but I was too young to understand it. I've been told that it's intoxicating beyond my wildest dreams. Women only love children and grandchildren, and that still doesn't come close to the love a man can feel for a woman. I wish I

could feel that kind of love. The best a man can hope for is respect from a woman. Most men don't know this or they would just give up on us. Men often die shortly after the loss of their mate—men can die from grief. Women, however, frequently live on for years after losing theirs."
Millie H. 52
wife/mother/author

"I hate a successful woman that acts happy because it magnifies my failures and my dependence on a man. She's, like, making fun of me because I'm married."
Renetta A. 38
office worker

"We are nasty, conniving, and cutthroat even when we're young. The older, more educated women are the worst. They're our real competition."
Stephanie K. 43
jewelry maker

"Cougars have ruined it for younger women. They have money, and they'll do everything for a man that we won't do, like swallow. My brother is banging a cougar twice his age and she gave him a new pickup."
Maddy E. 21
student

"Have you ever noticed that the blondes with tiny little bodies and plastic boobs always drive the nicest cars? They always have a huge diamond on their finger. They know what men want and they bust ass to give it to them. They're not stupid or lazy. They're either exploiting a man, or bringing out the best in him. They don't have an eating disorder, now do they? I hate every last one of them."
Patricia H. 44
waitress

"What do women want?—you *dumbshit!* We don't have a clue what we want!"
Belinda Y. 34
massage therapist

3 at war with each other

"A woman who thinks she's got it all is a bleeding wound, and other women are sharks—there *will* be a feeding frenzy."
   Rita O. 39
   office manager

"I hate it when she brags about how happy she is with her husband. I wanna fuck him just once and have her catch us."
   Jenny B. 27
   college student

"Women used to hide their problems to maintain some dignity. Now we can't wait to get to work to share every single thing that happens at home. And if we have a good relationship, we'll make shit up just to fit in. If we don't complain to the other women we know, they'll sabotage us. But you know what?—even though our problems are a lie, we start believing it and then we take it out on our husbands. We go home mad."
   Kathy A. 36
   collections agent

"Why be with a good man, when women will stop at nothing to get him in bed?—way too much stress."
   Mary J. 28
   high-school counselor

"I guess it's because we love doom. We give our friends the power to end our relationship with a man, and then we blame the man!"
Sarah W. 33
title officer

"I only sleep with married men. It's all fun and no work. The women who say their married boyfriend will leave his wife are lying to themselves. If he did leave his wife, they would freak out. They don't want the responsibilities—let the wife raise the monster kids and clean the damn toilet."
Christy T. 38
middle-school teacher

"Every time I do a guy I leave something behind, like an earring or my thong. I hide it where I know she'll find it—a *lot* of women mark their territory. One time I was doing a married man in his pickup and I didn't have earrings on, and I hadn't taken my jeans all the way off. So I pulled out some of my blonde hair and wrapped it around the door handle when he wasn't looking. His wife was a brunette."
Sandy M. 23
living with parents

"When I was in college I joined a group of nine other women called 'The Credit Card Club.' We knew that women were treating their men like shit, so we decided to cash in on it. We only slept with married men who had credit cards with a high limit. We met every day in the cafeteria to compare what they bought for us. This diamond bracelet was my last score—cool, huh?"
Ruth G. 31
medical technician

"When I'm bored and I need to get laid, I look for a wedding ring on a man before I turn on the charm. Having sex with a married man does two things—you get laid, and you screw with another woman's mind."
Vicky J. 39
court reporter

"I work with seventy-five women. I went on a date with this guy who was a pilot. On our first date he flew me to the beach and took me horseback riding—it was a dream date. When he took me home, he kissed me on the cheek and didn't even try to sleep with me. I

took pictures at the beach of the airplane and the horses, and put them on my desk at work. When my co-workers saw the photos they warned me to be careful or someone would steal him from me. They kept asking me if he had a brother—they were drooling! He started picking me up at work to take me to lunch and when I came into the reception area, there were always at least three of my co-workers around him, flipping their hair like schoolgirls. So I dumped him."
Laura A. 39
office worker

"When I'm at a nightclub or a bar, I don't care who hits on me—what I care about is the women who *see* him hitting on me. Now *that's* competition!"
Deanna W. 37
single parent/exotic dancer

"How do I fuck with other women?—okay, let's say I'm at a party with a bunch of other couples. I pick a man out of the crowd and start making eyes at him. He feels special and his fucking testosterone goes through the roof, and he ignores his bitch wife. I'll fuck with him for hours. What he doesn't know is, I could give a shit about him. The poor bastard doesn't have a clue that I'm *really* fucking with his skinny wife who treats him like shit. *Touché,* mother-fuckers!"
Hillary H. 31
convenience store clerk

"The best way to kick another woman's ass is to show more tit, have sex with her guy in the back seat of the car *in the parking lot,* and promise him anything. It works every time."
Olivia I. 46
bartender

"There are still a lot of good men out there, but women have decided that they are *all* assholes. I hear it all the time. You know what women have done?—they've adopted what they believe from other women rather than figuring it out for themselves. Personally, I prefer to decide for myself what I believe, and I don't let a group do it for me."
Carolina H. 34
office worker

"American women cross the border on the weekend and go to the cantinas. They get drunk and take off their clothes for everybody. I hate it when my husband goes out. In Spanish, we call a machete a 'gringa'—a white girl—because they cut families to pieces."
Delia G. 44
housewife/mother

"I married an American because I wanted to have beautiful children and security, and I respect my husband. I don't want to be a liberated American woman. One day all the happy women will be from other countries and American women will be our housekeepers. America is full of good men if you know how to be a good woman."
Katia S. 37
housewife/mother

"I fucking *hate* foreign women. My husband works with two of them and he can't stop talking about how they act. He says they're not sleazy like the other women in his office. I think they should all be, like, deported."
Margi Y. 26
insurance agent

"Why do we call ourselves bitches?—because we say and do things that a female dog would be ashamed of. Any more questions?"
Inez G. 35
bank teller

"A bitch at sixteen is a bitch at sixty. Once a woman has benefited from throwing a fit to get what she wants, she'll never change."
Beatrice H. 74
retired schoolteacher

"I warned my son to stay away from the pretty girls. Their heads are full of nothing but getting attention from men. They're useless to a good man and they *will* sleep with your best friend."
Lois F. 50
horse breeder

"If we talk about being happy with our life, we'll be attacked by everybody at work."
Deborah P. 42
receptionist

3 AT WAR WITH EACH OTHER

"I'm dating a really great guy and we decided to wait to have sex. All the girls at work ask me every morning 'Well, did you get laid yet?' When I remind them that we're waiting, they ridicule me and say 'Oh, yeah—he's gay.'"
Darla H. 47
movie theater manager

"We tell a new employee that if she's going to work here, she has to come with us for *girl's night out*. We go to bars and clubs just to get away from the men. Tiffany was a really young newlywed married to a terrific guy with a good job. They just bought a house and they both loved their in-laws. She drove a brand new SUV and we hated her because her life was so perfect. Her husband let her go out with us, and on the second weekend she got blasted and ended up in a motel room with some guy from the bar, and didn't get home until the next morning. Her husband divorced her and she quit her job."
Candice Y. 41
office worker

"All it takes is one miserable woman to infect an office full of them with her misery. Her goal is to make sure there are no happy women in the office. She gets them all to doubt their husband's dedication and fidelity, and before long there are divorces! I've watched it happen for twenty years."
Marge T. 57
financial auditor

"It's true—we *are* vindictive. There's no such thing as a female friend. We hang out together, but we know that our *'friends'* can turn on us in a second. It's the law of the jungle. They'll lie to you, do your boyfriend, break up your marriage, and then *after* lunch..."
Greta T. 37
vocational financial aid

"Women say they hate men because they're assholes, but they're just saying what other women want to hear. Really, they hate other women and put their anger on men, so they don't get caught hating women. Women hate each other way more than they hate men—*Denial!* Women are cutthroat and competitive, and they will destroy themselves before they'll admit it."
Edda W. 57
nurse

"I have a girlfriend who's really overweight and I take her to the bar on the weekends. She thinks I like her company, but I just use her to make *me* look thin. I use her for contrast and it works. I always get asked to dance first, and I always go home with a guy first. That's why we always take her car—if nobody hits on her, she has a way home."

Irma V. 46
city parks worker

"I met this guy and I introduced him to my friends at an open house I hosted. They all snubbed him except for my friend Cathy. She was very pretty for forty-six, and she couldn't stay away from him. When she found out that he repaired computers, she invited him to come to her house to have a look at hers. He was such a gentleman and told her to bring the computer to my house and he'd have a look at it. She kept insisting that he come to her house. He refused, and she got mad at *me!* The bitch was married and she wanted to get my boyfriend alone. And they say that *men* are assholes?"

Dedra O. 53
retail store owner

"If you started a dating site just for good women looking for good men, the only ones who would sign up would be whores and gold-diggers in pigtails. They're wolves in sheep's clothing. Just the mention of a good man, especially one that has a job and a house, attracts the vultures. Maybe we should start a website like that and use it as a man's guide to avoiding dangerous women."

Ivy O. 61
animal lover

"Women should be *for* each other, not against each other. But that's our world."

Ginger A. 34
shipping dispatcher

4 behind every man..?

"Behind every successful man is a good woman—if you say that at work, you'll get knifed. Women won't accept that they could be the reason a man might succeed."
Betty T. 64
business owner

"The best men in the world are built by women, and that's a fact. I know a lot of very successful and important men, and not one of them would deny that their wife was the reason for their success. It's nature—delegating each role to the person most capable of filling it. Women need to wise up."
Naomi T. 47
regional political consultant

"Men don't have a chance in hell of finding a decent girl. I'd hate to be a man in this society!"
Cameron R. 38
wedding planner

"Men are so easy to control—just dress sleazy and get them to talk about themselves. It makes them feel important, and they'll think you're Cinderella. I'm so bad, but it's true!"
Annie M. 23
temp service

"The knowledge about how to run the world has always been in the hands of women. Any woman has the ability to talk a man into—or out of—his throne. She can start a war, big or small, just by complaining to a man. But don't forget, war is fun to the woman who started it."
> *Elizabeth C. 24*
> *university history major*

"Women have always had the power to make a man the best he can be. We just don't take the time to pick a good one. We'd rather fight with them. Why is that? Maybe it's so other women won't want them. Jesus!—women are messed-up!"
> *Rosalba E. 36*
> *bank teller*

"Years ago we had the advantage over men. Men knew it, but we didn't abuse it. We could choose any man we wanted, but we made him work so hard to get our attention. We insisted on respect because we were concerned about our futures, and there was a discipline about it. We called it courting. It drove off the men who went to the bad part of town, and we were better-off for it. *My lord*, but the tables have turned. My daughter said my grandson can make a cell-phone call and have any number of young girls drive to his apartment and—well, I'd rather not say. We were trying to be honorable, but honor has gone out the window."
> *Margaret D. 82*
> *widow/retired*

"A man has it made because women are so loose, he can get laid every day by a different woman. It's our fault—we taught them that we're all whores. How could I get a man to believe I'm different without lying?"
> *Linda H. 44*
> *personal trainer*

"So many [American] women have sex. That's bad for men if they're looking for a girlfriend. That's why so many men get wives from other countries. I don't blame them. If a man asks me about American women, I tell them to run away. I have a sister who wants a good husband."
> *Nora H. 51*
> *retail clerk*

"I can spot a miserable guy a mile away. If he's got a ring on, he's being mistreated by a woman. I can have my way with him—I just treat him nice."
Sue W. 47
aerobics instructor

"We are so stupid! Men have *allowed* us to become the new slave workforce and we volunteered to do it—sneaky bastards! They let us think that we're their equals. We still don't make enough to replace them, but we sure do believe we can. *Oooh,* look at me, I have a job and a car—big fucking deal! Who else is paying your bills? Every damn one of us gripes about wanting a man to take care of us, but most of us are too fucked-up to make it happen. We just aren't motivated."
Angela Z. 19
college student

"Men don't have a mid-life crisis—the mid-life crisis is his wife! If a man goes crazy at forty, it's because he can't handle the bitch he's married to, and I've known plenty of them. I even slept with a few of their husbands. Is that wrong? He feels guilty, when she's really the guilty one for treating him like shit and cutting him off in bed."
Asia F. 32
vocational career counselor

"It's the beating of the drum—men beat the drum, and we'll go anywhere with them if they expose us to something we can brag about to our friends. The bragging always includes sleeping with him. The band members at a bar have their pick of any girl in the place after the last set. I've watched the girls hover around them like flies. If a guy has a cool hobby, we let him have his way with us for bragging rights. Women act like they hate a man, but they'll do anything for him, even if he's taking a different girl to bed every night. Whose fault is that? I make myself sick."
Paula E. 29
food server

"Men are just a utility—a means to an end. Women have taken this man-bashing thing way too far, and men are changing because of it. Men are bitter and starting to lose their respect for women."
Laurie H. 53
social worker

"If a man is looking for a nice girl, he's screwed—because all women act nice at first. How's the poor bastard supposed to tell the difference? He thinks he has a choice, but he really doesn't unless he's a psychic."

Allie K. 24
office manager

"Men are so fucking gullible I can make them believe anything. I can get caught in the act and still talk a man out of what he saw, and he'll feel bad about it and apologize. *Damn,* I'm good!"

Sonya N. 28
911 dispatcher

"I go to bars for free drinks. If I dress right, I can drink myself stupid and never pay for a drink. I never take money to a bar. You know what I do?—I put the straw from every drink I get in my purse so that later I'll know how much I drank. So I wake up naked every now and then with some cowboy I don't even know—at least the drinks were free!"

Cathy O. 54
accountant

"I hate pleasers! They go to bars to meet women, thinking they're going to start some kind of a meaningful relationship. Most times you can spot them, but not always. They try way too hard to fit in, and they think you'll spend the whole night with them—*Wrong!* Then they want your number to call you, like you're already married. I always give a fake number. They need to stay out of the bars. My brother is a pleaser and I always tell him he treats women way too good."

Natalie R. 36
receptionist

"I work with a lot of men and they always tell me their woman problems, like I'm supposed to have the answers. I tell them all the same thing—'Get the bitch off the pedestal and quit doing what she wants!' The more you give a woman, the more she wants. She'll never be satisfied. The poor bastards never get it, though."

Lynn P. 58
telemarketing

"The economy will give men back their rightful place. Men are survivors and providers, but they need a good reason to be. They can work harder than us, longer than us, and with more dedication if they have someone worthwhile to do it for. Women's jobs are too dependent on the economy and their little two-year degrees. Hardworking men will be in demand sooner than you think, and smart women will be hunting for one. All most women do is gripe, and that's like fingernails on a chalkboard. They'll act surprised when another woman steals their husband or boyfriend. I love it! If they don't treat him nice, someone else will."

Marsha I. 62
convenience store owner

"Here's how it works: If a woman starts dating a man and he's really hot, he's fair game to her friends. If he's *really* hot, she won't waste any time showing him off. Then her best friend tries to do him, and if he doesn't cheat on her, he'll tell her what happened. Then he's really screwed! Even if she believes he turned down a piece of ass from her best friend, she'll act like it's his fault for coming on to her friend, and that saves her friendship. Do you get it *now?*"

Cassandra P. 31
dental assistant

"I have a friend who's a well-known surgeon with a huge house on the golf course, three very expensive cars, and a Buick. He also rents an apartment that he takes his dates to—in the Buick. Every woman asks him on the first date what he does for a living. He tells them he's a medical technician at the hospital. He's looking for someone to love him for who he is, not for what he does or how much money he has. Don't tell *me* men are stupid!"

Penny J. 52
signmaker

"Men are really passionate, and we have that effect on them. Not just about sex, but if we treat them right and value ourselves, they can be passionate about everything. Like buying a house for us, fathering children, and helping us reach our goals. When men stray, we need to look at ourselves for what we did to kill their passion. We want to break a man's spirit after we get our hooks in him, and we don't even know why we do it. I know why—to fit in with our miserable friends and our mothers. We're not passionate, we're greedy—so, shoot me!"

Leslie M. 49
real estate agent

"I feel sorry for American men because they need love and respect, but they can't get it from their women. If you love a man the right way he will give you everything you need. He will be proud because of his wife."
Anastasia G. 22
exchange student

"Men are not afraid of commitment! They're afraid of how we act, and they should be. How is a man supposed to find a good woman if we're all acting crazy? How can we blame men, when we act like raving lunatics?"
Ginger A. 49
hotel manager

"Men aren't afraid to commit—they aren't afraid of anything! Just because they get screwed-over by a bunch of hateful women and finally learn something, we call them afraid. What does that say about us? We watch men learn something and we want to call it a phobia? Could it be that we don't want them to learn, because then we won't have anyone to screw over?"
Michelle J. 37
art gallery director

"I was thinking about why everybody says they'd rather work with men, because women will stab you in the back. What does that make men?—better, right? If men are better, why do we treat them so bad?"
Felicia V. 35
office worker

"Women bitch about men who want sex at night, like they didn't earn it. *Ladies!*—sex is not currency! If you use sex as currency you're a goddamn hooker and you deserve to be treated like one! Women act appalled that he wants sex, even after an argument. Think about it—what's more futile than arguing with a woman? A man never wins! His best hope is to call a truce at night and make you feel good. Sex is his last hope. If you get *your* way, other women can see it in him at work the next day. They know what you did to him last night. They're sharks, and your next argument will be about why he smells like perfume. Stupid bitches!"
Milly U. 54
sheriff's deputy

"Women can't make enough money to pay for a second car and childcare. And anyway, who's going to cook the meals and run the house? But it's a woman's right to work, and if he has anything to say about it, he's controlling. The only reason most married women work is to hang out with other women they hate anyway. If I were a man I'd kill myself."

Andrea W. 41
working mother

"If a woman thinks men are all a bunch of assholes, it's because she picked one on purpose and married him. Chances are that he had potential, but she made him an asshole by mistreating him. That should be the definition of 'asshole'—a man who reacts to being treated like shit."

Winona D. 54
human resources

"If men are so shitty, why are they the best at everything? They're the best chefs, hairstylists, cosmetic surgeons—a man even invented cosmetics! And brassieres! And if our car breaks, we sure the *fuck* don't call a girlfriend to bring her tools! Everybody I know would rather go to a man for anything. Maybe that's why we hate them—because we always need one."

Julie L. 25
unemployed

"The best way to a get a decent man's attention is by dressing properly. That's my job—teaching women how to dress. My first lesson is teaching them that hanging their tits in the wind just gets them bedded, not married. They have a hard time understanding that covered breasts are far more alluring than bare ones. If they have the guts to want a doctor or a lawyer, I put them in a pleated tea-length skirt, no cleavage showing, round-toe medium heels, light makeup, tiny earrings—not hoops—and their hair pulled back with a simple clip. It drives men out of their minds! The bad boys won't even approach them, but the successful men come running. I take them to a lounge in a nice restaurant and make them order a soda. It's pure magic to see it work. Now I just wish I could teach them how to behave."

Huda W. 50
designer/consultant

"A guy in his fifties with a car, a job, and a credit card can get laid anytime he wants by a ton of desperate women half his age. That's about the time in a marriage when a woman has perfected the art of being a raging bitch. Do the math."
Liz B. 43
retired military

"I feel bad for the men looking for a wife. All women seem like potential life partners because the bad ones act just like the good ones in the beginning. Sometimes a man doesn't really know her until after the wedding, and then it's too late. If I were a man looking for a respectable woman to marry, I'd hire a female private investigator to befriend her and get the truth first. You know, they really do that. A lot of women hire a P.I. to hit on their fiancé, to see what he will do. Men should do it too."
Isabelle Q. 47
piano teacher

"Most women just watch other people do things. Men actually *do* things. We're just an audience waiting for men to entertain us. I like water skiing, but I've never owned a boat. I like flying, but I don't know how to fly. What else?—I like scuba diving, but I'll probably never go unless I date a guy who does it. Yup, just an audience."
Donna Y. 32
retail clerk

"The men I work with are totally confused about women. They think because all the women they go out with want to have sex immediately, they're all whores. They're right—they *are* whores."
Elizabeth N. 56
county auditor

5 the war against men

"If you want something from a man, just throw a fit, ignore him, and cut him off in bed—he'll cave in."
Tanya H. 27
concessions

"I hate the way I treat men, but it's the only way to get what you want. Well, isn't it?"
Keeky T. 26
psychology student

"Have you watched TV lately? The commercials and sitcoms all treat men like they're stupid. I think we get brainwashed to think the same thing about all men. It's not even our idea. No, really!—look for it next time you watch TV."
Mandy N. 17
student

"I hate it when women say 'It must be a guy thing,' like they just had an epiphany about men. To call anything a 'guy thing' is just proof of their ignorance about men and a lack of desire to learn about them. It's like calling your husband's part of the house a 'man cave'—it's demeaning."
Mary G. 46
office worker

"My fiancé is sixteen years older than me. He's not very good looking, but he has a good job with retirement. Should I feel bad that I don't love him? I mean, he's lucky to have me when I'm so young, right? I'm thinking about security and he gets a beautiful young wife to show off. Anyway, if we get divorced I'll get some of his retirement."

Jeri S. 21
unemployed

"Those poor bastards. We accuse them of rape, sexual harassment, molestation and mental abuse, and everyone believes us! If you piss me off, I can burn you down. It's a great way to end a relationship. It's all based on our misery with being in the workplace instead of in a happy home. We live to make sure our men don't have any peace-of-mind."

Hanna Y. 32
pizza delivery

"Oh, I was a bitch when I was married. I hated him for no reason. One time I was in the middle of chewing his ass and I had to go to the bathroom. While I was gone, he got in the car and drove off. *Ohhh, no!*—nobody drives off in the middle of *my* argument. If I started it, goddamnit, I'm going to finish it! I was so pissed-off I started pinching myself—I mean really hard, too. When I was all bruised-up I called the cops and told them he beat me. They took pictures of my bruises and went to arrest him. I fucked up, though—I forgot that I'd told him I did the same thing to my stepmother when I was thirteen. The cops called my stepmother and she sold me out and saved his ass. I'll get even one day."

Suzy C. 36
gold-digger ("Well, that's what I am.")

"Sure, I'm a bitch. But I can turn it on, and I can turn it off. Scary, huh?"

Lisa D. 24
property management

"We're all crazy! We were born with femininity and we're all trying to be men! If you find yourself complaining about having to do housework, cooking, raising the kids, and holding down a full time job, y'all are living way beyond your means. And who always sets the standard?—the greedy woman trying to impress her friends. Men don't have less responsibility, just fewer responsibilities. But their workload is bigger because they were built for it, and we weren't. Now we're a major part of the workforce, but all we do is complain about it and secretly look for a way to get free of it."

Betty M. 59
housewife/mother

"Guys who go to bars to meet women deserve what they get. I mean, really—they're just a bunch of sleaze-bags! If they hook up with some girl early, they're the lucky ones. If they hook up late, it's because they were our last choice. We go to bars to practice our style. Oh, yeah—and get free drinks, too."

Sophia D. 26
barista

"It's hard work being so complicated. We can't risk being understood because if we were, we'd be powerless against men. It's better to keep them guessing whether they're doing the right thing or not."

Trish F. 34
city employee

"Just because we need a man doesn't mean we can't live without them. If I could afford to support myself, I would buy the most expensive vibrator in the world and never speak to another man again—no offense."

Jana R. 28
cable TV sales

"I was really heavy when I was married—okay, fat! I was eating everything that wasn't glued down. I was even buying food and hiding it so my husband wouldn't know how much I was eating. One day he was at work and I spent the whole day stuffing myself. That night I was so constipated I thought I was going to die. It was late and all the stores were closed so he took apart a ballpoint pen, stuck it on a bottle of baby oil, and gave me an enema. It worked! When I ended it with him I needed to explain why I left such a great guy, so I told everybody he was a pervert and he liked to stick things up my butt."

Libby A. 48
receptionist

"Your ex-girlfriend is dating a cop? Here's what you do—find out what his name is, give me a time and a date, and hide in the dumpster behind the mall with your camera. When the patrol car pulls up, get ready to take some really damning pictures with me giving him a blowjob in uniform. Trust me—she'll quit dating him when he gets fired."

 Bonnie B. 33

 prostitute

"When my ex-husband got remarried I didn't want my kids around his new wife, so I started sleeping with a cop and got him arrested. I let him take the kids out-of-state and called my new cop boyfriend. My ex had a paper that I'd signed giving him permission to take our kids out-of-state, but I convinced my cop that he should arrest my ex, and he finally did. The charges were dropped the next day because of the paper I signed, but I got his ass thrown in jail for a few hours. I win!"

 Kim O. 44

 cocktail waitress

"Our female ancestors fought along *with* men for our freedom, and some of their men and sons were sacrificed for that freedom. Good women were full of fight. Now most of us are bleeding-heart liberals voting to disarm our men. Spoiling for a fight is great until we fight *against* our own men. How pitiful can we get?"

 Lori E. 54

 high-school teacher

"My husband is a total pussy. He's always worried about bills and the budget. If I want a new dress I buy it, take the tags off, and throw it in the clothes hamper for a week. Then I wash it and when he sees me in it, he asks me 'Is that a new dress?' I yell at him 'Damnit, Rob!—you never pay attention to me! You treat me like I'm invisible!' I didn't really lie to him. He's sorry, and he acts like he remembers seeing the dress before."

 J.J. W. 33

 billing agent

"I met my husband at the bar on a Friday night after work, and we drank too much. I went home, but he wanted to stay a little longer. After an hour I started to worry, so I went looking for him. When I walked in the bar, a friend's wife had taken her top off and had just sat on my husband's lap. I could tell he was shocked by it, but I was pissed-off anyway. I promised him I'd get even, and I did. Four years later I arranged for him to find me in bed with one of our young employees. When he freaked out, I said 'Remember the bar?' I'm a woman and I can hold a grudge. No, it wasn't his fault, but I got even with her by punishing him. Now he hates her too."

Taylor S. 52
restaurateur

"We'll do anything to get attention from a man, even if it's horrible. Not getting attention is, like, the most boring thing in the world."

Annie M. 24
family business

"I dated a wonderful man who was a single parent of a 15-year-old daughter. She started sneaking out at night to go to parties. He put an alarm on her door and window, and threatened to call the police if she did it again. So she told a school counselor that her father was molesting her. He was arrested, lost his job as a city official, and his daughter became a ward of the state. I saw how the little bitch treated him, and I would have beat her within an inch of her life. He avoided prison, but he never got his job or his daughter back. I think he's better off. There were months of legal proceedings and his daughter eventually recanted, but it was too late."

Cynthia G. 41
graphic artist

"If men knew how far a woman will go to get the best of them, they'd all be gay. If my boyfriend is winning an argument I push him and threaten to call the police. I try to get him to hit me, even though I know he never would. He gets scared, and I win."

Ginny C. 41
art director

"My mom and dad were divorced before I was born, and I had to listen to her totally trash my dad my whole life. My mom always made fun of him. She even made fun of the way he did dishes. I had to think the way my mom did, so I made fun of him too. But you know what?—my dad was always my hero. I don't see my dad anymore. I guess he got fed up with us."

Nicole T. 27
waitress

"Men should never be completely naked. A naked woman is a work of art, but a man's genitals are gross. I'd rather look at a naked woman any day."
Inez V. 35
court reporter

"If a man gets successful after a few years of marriage, we get scared. We liked him better as a loser. I hate a confident man. I'll sleep with him, but I don't want to compete with him. Wait, it's really the women I don't want to compete with. Which women?—the ones who will want him now that he's somebody. The only thing to do is to dump him, take him for everything he's worth, and find another loser. Then I'm in control again."
Rosaline U. 39
certified counselor

"It's always the man's fault anymore. I hear it all day long at work. I never hear a woman telling a story about how she did something wrong."
Hilda L. 61
office worker

"Oh, my god!—you wouldn't believe how many new boyfriends I've had. I usually hook up with a guy from out-of-town because I've been in bed with just about every guy where I live, and it's awkward to run into all the guys I slept with. When I get bored I break up with them, and I cry to my family to get me back home. I have to tell big fat lies to make me look like the victim—that's the only way to get my mom to send me money. It's just what I do."
Kit N. 41
unemployed

"I was fighting with my husband, and it was bad. What did he do?—nothing really, I was just mad. Does a woman need a reason? Anyway, I started throwing things and breaking things. This went on for over an hour. The more he tried to calm me down, the madder I got. I couldn't get him to fight. He always kept his pistol in the nightstand, and for some reason I opened the drawer. *No!*—I swear I wasn't going to shoot him. Anyway, the pistol was gone. He hid it because I was acting so crazy. So I screamed at him *'Where's the pistol?!'* and he turned white as a sheet. You should have seen his face. He wouldn't tell me where it was, so I locked myself in the

bathroom and turned on the water so he couldn't hear me calling 911. I told them he was going to kill himself, and five police cars, an ambulance, and a hostage negotiator all showed up. They took his pistol and interviewed him for an hour about why he wanted to kill himself."
Frannie A. 43
unemployed

"When my little sister was eighteen she hated working. My husband and I had a friend who was making a ton of money, and my sister set her sights on him. He was fourteen years older than her and he'd just gone through a divorce. My sister had him by the balls in nothing flat. She treated him really good for about a year, and then she encouraged him to accept a job offer out-of-state for a lot more money. Of course he did, and they moved. She was six weeks pregnant by this time. I felt so bad because I knew what she was going to do to him, but I couldn't go against my sister. They moved into their new apartment and before he had a chance to report for his new job, she called our mom for a plane ticket to fly back home and leave him there. I thought he was going to die. My sister's plan was to come back home, collect welfare and a get a big child-support check from him every month. You know what he did?—he rented another truck and followed her home. I felt so bad for him because he really loved her, but I had to laugh at her because her stupid plan didn't work."
Jessica H. 54
hairstylist

"Women are so sexist it isn't funny. There are all kinds of bad people on this planet, but if we hear a story about one bad man we decide that all men are like that. There are also bad women who break up marriages, kill their husbands, and drown their kids. Why don't women hear a story like that and say 'All *women* are assholes?' They're more likely to blame a man for making them do it."
Petra H. 47
city mayor

"Oh, *fuck* yeah!—if a woman treated my brother like I treat men, I'd tell him to slap the bitch across the room!"
Lori S. 38
CPA

"I can lure a man into a relationship, totally destroy his ego and self-esteem, and I feel nothing—just power. It makes me feel alive."
Belinda G. 35
organic produce vendor

"I don't destroy all men. We have this friend who really deserves a great gal in his life, but he doesn't have a clue about how women really are. He says he wants to find a woman he can have an intellectual conversation with. I warned him that if he finds a smart woman she'll just use it to exploit and destroy him. See, I have some compassion."
Nancy N. 35
real estate agent

"Men become disgusting about six months after the relationship starts. I got my wedding, my honeymoon, and now I'm knocked-up, so he needs to shut the fuck up and work."
Gina J. 26
refuses to work

"You don't know about a turkey baster? It's a tube-like thing with a rubber ball at one end so you can suck up the juice and squirt it on the turkey—like a big eyedropper. I guess it keeps the turkey from getting dry. So if you want a baby and a check, you hit on a guy that's got a really good job. You tell him you're on your period and you just want him to feel good. You give him a blowjob, excuse yourself, and he thinks you're going to the bathroom to spit and rinse. You spit it into the turkey baster and inject it into your hoo-ha. When the paternity papers are served, he has no memory of fathering a child with you. Cha-ching!"
Cecilia I. 31
temp service

"My good friend raised his daughter by himself for nine years. He got custody of her when she was six years old because his wife decided to trade her registered-nursing certificate for a life of meth addiction. He was the best father I've ever seen, and she was the brightest, most polite daughter any parent could hope to have. When her breasts developed she wanted to dress like a barfly, and her dad would have nothing to do with it. She became the most hateful person, and she displayed her disgust for her father's authority every day. He tried everything he could to get through to her, but nothing worked. The battle raged for two years, until one day she made a veiled threat to accuse him of touching her inappropriately if he didn't let her dress the way she wanted. She was fifteen years old then. He put her on a plane on Christmas day and sent her to her meth-addict mother who started her on birth control and allowed her be the whore she wanted to be. She posted pictures of her adolescent sexual escapades and drinking on the internet. It's been eight years since he sent her away, but he will never be right because of it. I know her mother, and she is delighted at the outcome."

Chrissy H. 39
makeup artist

"My daddy was strict and he was always worried about his four girls. I guess it was good that he cared about us, but he always got in our way and he drove us nuts. When we wanted to do something that he wouldn't approve of, me and my mom would make Daddy a milkshake. When he heard the blender going his mouth would water. He didn't know that we put three or four muscle-relaxers in it. Pretty soon he'd start yawning and slip away for a short nap. Maybe eighteen hours later when he woke up, he'd always say 'Man, I must have been tired!'"

Louisa H . 27
fast-food worker

"I left my husband and married my mom's next-door neighbor. My ex made a great babysitter. He was alone and he really loved our 5-year-old son. Then he found a girlfriend—*Game over!* She might have been a nice person, but my son wasn't going to love any woman but me! While my ex and his bimbo were engaged, I got a written excuse from a different doctor every two weeks so he couldn't see our son. When they got married I accused him of molesting our son. That stopped visitation for months, until he took a polygraph test and passed. Then they made me take one to see if I had made it up, and I failed. So I talked my new husband into moving us across-country. My ex never saw his son again. Why did I do it?—I knew his new wife was better than me, and you don't fuck with a woman's children!"

Clarice H. 32
food server

"If we start dating and you accidentally turn out to be a good guy, you're fucked! I'll claw your eyes out."

Barbara P. 47
laundry service worker

"I hated my husband because he always forgave me. When we were engaged I wigged out and broke up with him five different times, and he still married me. Why did I marry him?—I knew he was the best choice for a husband, but I also knew it wouldn't last because I'm such a bitch. I was mad when I broke up with him all those times, but I was more mad when he took me back. I just hid it at first. And when I married him it was just to get even with him for being so stupid."

Jean P. 43
business owner

"I treat my husband like shit all the time! It keeps him in line, and it keeps him guessing. That's how you control a man, don't you know?"

Elisa S. 57
city controller

"I catch myself doing it all the time—I talk to my husband like he's a stupid dog. I hate that about myself, but I can't stop!"

Nancy W. 28
personal secretary

"I think this is the same topic. My ex-husband was a bodybuilder and other than being able to lift heavy stuff, he was useless. He had girls hitting on him all the time and I was getting fat. We finally got divorced, but I still have pictures of him weightlifting. You know what I do when I start dating a new guy?—I start showing him pictures of my daughter and my family, and I sneak in some pictures of my ex. Why do I do this? I even told one guy that I'm more used to muscle guys. I can't believe I would say that to a man. Do I want to make them feel inadequate?"

Susan R. 31
communications

"You know what I don't get?—why we feel the need to compete with men. We get all pumped-up to be better than a man, and we always fail. The only way to feel better is to make *them* fail. My husband opened two very successful businesses for us, and I destroyed both of them. I know he did it for me, but he was also proud of himself. I think I wanted him to be a loser or something like that. If he's doing good, I look like a fat loser."

Wendy R. 44
church secretary

"If we're going to attack a man we have to make sure that we're smarter than him. If we try to attack a smart man, we'll get our asses kicked—and women are not good losers."

Cassie M. 27
financial aid officer

"I was dating a raging alcoholic when another man asked me out. He had a house, a business, an airplane *and* a boat, and he was a babe! I went out with him and he was a perfect gentleman. We were so compatible. We had the same sense of humor, he looked good and so did I. It was perfect and I couldn't handle it. After our date I accused him of being a player and said I knew what his game was. I saw him ten years later when I was married to the alcoholic and hating my life. I was eighty pounds heavier and he still treated me like I was the most beautiful woman in the world. I need therapy, don't I?"

Theresa V. 51
business owner

"I treat men like shit because if there is someone who has done something to be proud of, it's almost always a man. I haven't done shit with my life, and I hate being around men who have accomplishments. It makes me feel worthless. No, they don't ever say anything about it. I think it all by myself and try to hurt them."

Destiny E. 37
fast-food worker

"The most powerful weapon against a man is a false accusation. Who wouldn't believe that a man did any number of horrible things? Our justice system wants us to believe that everyone is innocent until proven guilty, but a man is always guilty, even if he's really innocent. Women rule the jury."

Marcella A. 46
attorney

"My husband said he wanted me to grow my hair long—*Fuck him!* If he wants long hair he can grow it his goddamn self."
    Lulu R. 26
    construction worker

"When I started competing with men, I imagined being a college graduate and making more than them. What a fucked-up delusion!"
    Julia Y. 38
    social worker

"The past is supposed to be the past, but I can't help it. I love to see the look on a man's face when I tell him that my last boyfriend took me to Costa Rica, or about the other date that took me sailing. It's a pissing contest and I like to wave my 'dick' around. If he wants to be with me, he needs to grow a pair."
    Kathy F. 43
    barista

"What's the worst thing I do on a date?—well, after sex I always work in the line 'That was great, but I've had bigger.' Is that hateful, or what?"
    Susanna O. 39
    catering

"I hate it when a man gives me a compliment. Whatever he likes about me now is headed straight for the floor. If he likes my perky boobs now, what's he going to think when I start tucking them in the elastic waistband of my polyester pants? I've seen what they're gonna look like. My mom is only seventeen years older than me, and her boobs look like foot-long raisins and her belly looks like a bowl of oatmeal. I'm already mad about it—so if you know what's good for you, don't compliment me."
    Virginia B. 39
    prison guard

"You want to know how fucked-up women are? I was in the mood for a fight and my husband recorded me while I was yelling at him. It made me want to kill him, but when he played it back to me I had to laugh. It started like this: I said 'You know what's wrong with you?—I'll *tell* you what's wrong with you—you always want to control everything!' He said 'Wait just a minute here, who decided where we were going to live? And who decided what kind of business we started? Oh, yeah—and who decided how we spent our tax return?' I said 'Well, maybe that's your problem then—you don't want to control anything!' How fucked-up is that?"

Lou H. 38
retail

"Men are so easy to control. I slept with two different attorneys to get my divorce to turn out my way. It didn't cost me a dime. If you think that's bad, I even slept with my doctor to get a free tummy-tuck. He got paid for it because he called it something different, and billed my insurance. Sex is better than money because you don't have to pay taxes on it."

Mare F. 32
social worker

"I hate men because they invented everything. Everything we do, everything we wear, everything we drive—even breast implants! I'm starting to wonder if we aren't being controlled by men."

Rayna R. 34
physician's assistant

"I always end up in bed with every man I come on to. I was at a nightclub and I decided to fuck the bartender. I told him so, but he didn't want to. I offered to fuck him three different times and he turned me down every time. That's when I got pissed! He was polite enough about it, but *nobody* turns me down. He was wiping down the bar, and I grabbed his wrists and braced my foot on the bar and pulled him over it—I had leverage. He started screaming for the bouncer, and before his face hit the floor the bouncer grabbed me. It probably was a good thing for his face."

Erin L. 37
taxi driver

"When my husband and I separated, I told his best friend that I'd been in love with him since the first day we met. He fell for it, and it got me out of town. When I was done with him I tried everything to get him to leave, but he wanted it to work out. I finally told him I had been a prostitute and I wasn't capable of loving him. He finally let me go without a fight. No, I wasn't really a prostitute, but I had to say something to get rid of him."

Kerry R. 36
court liaison

"I go totally crazy when my husband sleeps with another woman. When I find out about it I want to kill them both! When I have sex with another man, it feels different. I'm not being fair, huh?"
Mirelli W. 31
housewife

"I never should have married him. He was in the military and he had a great career, and he ended up being the best husband a girl could ever want. He thought I was the most beautiful woman in the world, and I hated it. The truth is, I'm a whore bartender and I have a lot of fuck-buddies. I never dreamed he was a decent guy. If I'd known I wouldn't have married him. I thought he was just another guy to have sex with. I don't know why I accepted his offer to marry me, I really don't. I am so fucked-up! I couldn't see myself growing old with him when there were so many hot guys to fuck. I had to end it, but he wasn't going to let me so I told him I was fucking several other guys. He went crazy and started crying. I tried to hold him, but when he jerked away I fell forward and broke my nose. I called the police, and later he was convicted of spousal abuse. I didn't mean for him to lose his career in the military. The cops told me to get a restraining order against him, so I did. I do feel guilty about it, though."
Kendra U. 27
bartender

"My son is a good man who married the most hateful woman. I warned him once, but I didn't press the issue. After a year of fighting and breaking up, she accused him of pushing her and she called the police. He was arrested and convicted of spousal abuse. He was on probation, ordered to go to anger management classes, and there was a restraining order against him as well. Days after the ordeal, he asked me to accompany him to retrieve his belongings. His attorney advised him to have a witness to ensure his protection. I was supposed to meet him at the house at 5:00 PM, and when I arrived he was already there. I was sick about it. He met me in the driveway and told me I wasn't needed because they were working out their differences, and everything would be fine. He was a grown man, so I drove away. They ended up in bed, and when they had finished she asked him if he wanted her to order a pizza. He thought it was a good idea. She put on her bra and panties and left the bedroom to call for the pizza. She dialed 911, set the phone down, and bolted out of the house screaming 'rape.' She ran a half-block to a convenience store in nothing but her underwear, where she called 911 again to tell her tale. Because he had just deposited his DNA in his wife, he was convicted of rape and spent a year in prison. He's now a convicted felon and a registered sex-offender. When he was released from prison he reconciled with his wife. I have nothing to do with either of them anymore."

Candice B. 62
business director

"I hated my husband because when we argued, he would always win. No, he really made more sense than me, but that ain't the point. I hated it because it made me look stupid. Hell, maybe I was! Anyway, when he won an argument this one day, I'd had enough. Our son was with relatives so I made the bastard sleep in our son's room on this tiny little kid's bed. He gave me a shitty smirk when he went into my son's room, and he went right to sleep! That really pissed me off, so I took my son's T-ball bat and hit him in the head as hard as I could. I was sure that I'd killed him because he was convulsing and twitching—I knocked the living shit out of him. I leaned the bat against the wall and pulled the door shut while he was convulsing. I guess I figured I'd deal with his death the next day. In the morning I was shocked to see him fumbling in the medicine cabinet for aspirin. The stupid bastard didn't have a clue why he had a headache. Yeah, we're divorced now."

Marcy W. 59
butcher

"The behaviors that American women display toward men transcend any form of prejudice known to history. Women have waged a civil war against their male compatriots, and for what? Try to imagine the outcome. It's the proverbial house divided! I reserve my right to leave the country, and I may have to one day."

Meredith F. 48
sociology professor

"We hate everything that used to be good about men. We're the ones who changed—not men."

Hila Y. 45
auto service clerk

6 psychotherapy

"What's wrong with women can't be addressed psychologically. Their behaviors are deliberate, calculated, and narcissistic. They don't stem from disorders or mental illness, and drug treatments are inappropriate and ineffective. The direction that women have taken is nothing but a distraction from the horrible choices they've made. They are wrong to think they can have everything they ever wanted. They are wrong to believe that morality and family values are outdated. Most of all they are wrong to collectively point their fingers at the male gender as the cause of their own misery. Men are not, nor have they ever been, responsible for the collective behaviors of women. Women have adopted their mindset from the most unreliable sources—the media and other uneducated women."
Donna B. 54
therapist

"It's a business, like anything else. The more case files I have on my desk, the more job security I have. Some patients with real mental-health issues are truly in need of treatment, but the majority are just whiners or drug addicts who refuse to accept responsibility for the consequences of their own decisions. It's a living, though."
Vera K. 37
counselor

"Almost everyone I knew in college started with a different major. You know why we changed to psychology?—because we were nutcases and couldn't afford therapy. We thought we could treat ourselves for free and get a degree at the same time. If a therapist tells you anything different, they're lying. I mean, really—if you're already a basket-case, what good is it to lock yourself in a cage with a bunch of other basket-cases? Most of us dropped out—others settled for counseling certificates. Only a few of us got our degrees. Now I sit and listen half the day to the laziest people in the world complaining about why their lives are dysfunctional, and why they think I should increase their dosage."

Marsha Q. 48
therapist

"Marriage counseling is a total scam. I went to counseling to get my dumbshit husband off my back. The only thing I accomplished was to make the counselor look as dumb as my husband! She believed anything I said, and it was all bullshit! I was ranting about shit like the toothpaste cap and his dirty clothes just to fill up the time. My poor husband looked like a deer in the headlights, because nothing I was yelling about had a fucking thing to do with why we went to counseling. I noticed that the angrier I got, the more she would pressure my husband for his role in our marital problems. I toyed with this for a while, and sure enough—when I got pissed she picked on my husband. Then I got territorial. If anybody's going to pick on my husband, it's going to be me! We stopped going and I've lightened up on him a little, but he still thinks I'm crazy. And that's the way it should be."

Vicky C. 34
teacher's aide

"I went to couples' therapy before I divorced my husband. He begged me to try to save our marriage, but I already knew I was leaving. We should never have been married—I don't know what I was thinking. I didn't love him—didn't even like him. Anyway, I went out of guilt. He was a good guy and he thought I walked on water, but the magic just wasn't there. I admitted that I'd made a mistake by marrying him and it was all my fault. What pissed me off was the therapist telling us 'Well, you know—it takes two,' and she insisted that my husband was at fault too. I told her over and over it was all me, and he was a good man. She wouldn't buy it and she wouldn't let it go. I finally stood up and let her have it. I said 'Look, you stupid bitch—it doesn't take two, it only takes one, and that's *me!* My husband did nothing wrong and he's kept his marriage vows. I'm fucking my old boyfriend because he inherited a fortune, and I want to go to Europe! How the fuck is that anybody's fault but mine?!' My husband helped me move out."

Shandi T. 28
elementary schoolteacher

"Do you know what's so sad about it?—the media and marketing firms have thwarted all the work our ancestors did to civilize humanity. At this rate, we'll be living in caves again. No psychology can fix this."

Tiffany A. 50
psychology professor

"If we had a famine we would see it and feel it—it would be tangible. War in the streets would be tangible, with fatal results. An infectious epidemic would cause alarm and panic. On the other hand, a cultural disease is more insidious. Selfishness is our cultural disease. The result will be an entire culture of people with no knowledge of a common morality, no societal structure to support family life, no stability. Loneliness is at the end of selfishness, and it's already affected millions."

Abigail S. 63
therapist

"I wanted a divorce, but my husband didn't. He talked me into going to a famous psychiatrist in Santa Barbara who had been on TV. He charged $250 for forty minutes. We drove three hours to his mansion in the mountains, and I mean this place was like a fancy French palace. We sat in his office and I lied for the entire forty minutes. My husband looked like a bulldog chewing on a wasp—I fucked up his whole day. The psychiatrist believed everything I said and told my husband he was the one with the problem."

Denise J. 27
fast-food worker

"Psychologists are lucky to even scratch the surface of a woman's psyche."

Libby Y. 51
therapist

"If a man refuses to seek counseling, he's often accused of being indifferent about the marriage. I ask women who make this accusation to recite their marriage vows to me. Most women are vague about what they promised. I ask them if their vows have been kept, and they usually don't want to hear this. A man is a proud being, and if he has enough faith in himself and his mate to repair their own problems, I applaud him. Too often a woman solicits my services in the hope that I will take her side. I don't have time for it."

Sally E. 67
therapist

"I don't tolerate 'I'm working on it,' or 'I'm trying.' They're just excuses. When I hear a woman say 'I'm not as bad as I used to be,' I want to choke her! 'Not *as* bad' is still bad. I like the analogy of the water and a drop of poison. If I offered you a tall glass of pure water you'd be happy to drink it, right? If I put one drop of poison in it, would you still drink it? How many drops of poison each day are women using to contaminate their marriages?—can a tiny drop be that bad? If her husband beat her every day for years and then cut back to only once a week, should we applaud him? Women had a natural gift to mold and nurture a family. Anymore, it's lost to most women, but they won't admit it."

Betty R. 56
therapist

"Counseling for infidelity?—*Fuck me!* Give it up. If one of you has bedded the pool boy or the secretary, it's over. The only benefit of counseling is to prolong the punishment of whoever screwed up. Trust me—a therapist will gladly help you do it. I speak from experience."

Rachel H. 33
printer

"The only people who hear more lies than a therapist are the police. A man has a hard time lying to me in front of his wife. His wife, however, will lie straight-faced in front of her husband. Then it turns into who's lying, instead of getting at the actual problems. Women can be nasty."

Sisi M. 45
marriage counselor

"Therapy is B.S. Going to therapy made me lie even more. I wanted our therapist to think I really had my shit together and didn't need therapy. Besides, who's going to say to a shrink 'I'm a hateful bitch and I like it?' It's all just a game."
Candi O. 22
waitress

"The best psychologist in the world is the owner of the personality. That's you, dummy! Therapy can't fix mean or stupid."
Bella W. 26
county employee

"Women love therapy. We can change our stories faster than any expert can think! If anyone thinks they're an authority on women, they'd have better luck being a weather man."
Stacy V. 41
registered nurse

"Women won't let anyone know what they're really thinking. If you think women tell the truth to a shrink, think again. A woman's thoughts are like a virus—they mutate to survive. Nobody will ever make sense of it."
Kari A. 33
bank manager

"Psychology has become so feminized that it's actually doing more harm than good. The mental-health industry is a sponge for government funding and entitlements. Yeah, it's a place for drug addicts to take a break from addiction and get legal meds, but you should hear the conversations in the break room."
Kasey L. 30
mental health records

"There's a book called the DSM of mental disorders that they use to diagnose a patient's condition. It's like a catalogue of stuff for people to get out of work and get disability money. They never tell a patient that they *aren't* mentally ill. They need to have active files to keep the money coming in. Mental illness has replaced self-discipline and personal achievement. They invent new disorders, and exploit the patients and the taxpayers."
Trisanna G. 24
mental health receptionist

"Let me read this to you: 'Before Sigmund Freud, psychologists were women. They were better known as mothers and grandmothers. They charged nothing for their services and they worked tirelessly. Their success rates were far better than modern psychologists. They specialized in child psychology and preparation for adulthood. They offered expert advice to young women on keeping and maintaining their self-worth. They also encouraged young women to hold out for a decent, good-hearted man. They were well-respected, and adult men saw to it.' What on Earth have we done to ourselves?"
Raquel R. 51
high-school counselor

"The only people who change are the ones who change themselves. It's an internal decision that's never been understood by any psychologist. It's like the origin of motivation—it's still a mystery and it can't be duplicated, taught, or put in a pill."
Mirea D. 25
psychology student

"I have serious jealousy problems, and my husband works with women. It got so bad I wanted to kill someone, so I threatened to kill myself. My husband was telling me he loved me and only me, but that made it worse. It was just a big tantrum, but I had to do something so I called the mental hospital and had them pick me up. I spent four months in a nuthouse with all kinds of other women who were no more mentally ill than I was. I was a 40-year-old spoiled brat who never had to do anything I didn't want to, and I was insanely jealous. I was diagnosed with Borderline Personality Disorder—the new name for bitches like me who don't like rules. I got a free place to stay, free food, and they gave me the poor-baby treatment. They taught me to blame my husband for everything, and said I needed to leave him. They *hated* men. There's nothing wrong with my husband, but I couldn't tell them that."
Patty K. 29
receptionist

"The practice of psychology is a farce. Psychologists are supposed to figure out what's going on inside a person who doesn't know herself? How can he know anything about a person by studying them for an hour a week in a little office? Any marriage counselor would advise you to get to know a person's friends and family before considering marriage, and to observe their work habits and how they treat strangers. Psychologists can't do that. They don't practice what they preach. If they did, no one could afford them. If you want to know what someone wants, pay attention to what they do—not what they say. People generally do what they want, even if it's harmful to themselves or others. Watching a patient sit in a chair for an hour accomplishes nothing."

Henrietta A. 53
psychologist's wife

"I used to think men were all assholes—my friends said it all the time. Once, I said it to my counselor without thinking. She asked me how many people were on the planet. I had no idea. She said 'Billions—and of those billions, how many are men?'—not a clue. She said 'Almost half are men and that's still billions, right?' *Okay, right!* Then she asked me 'How many of them do you know?—enough to decide they're all assholes?' I don't say it anymore."

Cheyenne P. 26
university student

"My uncle really loved his wife, but she left him for no reason—not one I knew of anyway. He convinced her to go to marriage counseling, and she did—just once. He told the counselor everything that was going on, and impressed him with a thorough explanation. Then the counselor said 'What are you going to do about it?' My uncle lost his words, and the counselor just sat there looking at him. My uncle spent $125 for 'What are you going to do about it?' Later my uncle said it was the best money he ever spent because he decided to do something about it."

Regina V. 33
motel manager

"Women are notorious for dragging their husbands to therapy for infidelity. What they don't get is that if they mistreat their husband, he *will* look for affection elsewhere. Most often it's the wife who drives him into the arms of another woman. When a woman doesn't like her husband, I'd like to say 'You picked him,' but I can't because it's not ethical. Goddamn ethics."

Geraldine Z. 49
marriage counselor

7 sex

"Sex with a guy for the first time is the best. You don't have to be a good lover because the excitement of the first time does all the work. I don't have the time or the desire to learn what makes a guy tick in bed. Let him find a wife for that."

Eva R. 23
golf course attendant

"Sex is romance or recreation for men. For women, it's currency. And believe me, we know how to spend it!"

Lindy V. 57
bus driver

"For twenty years I had sex with every man I could get my hands on. I've had sex in public restrooms, parking lots, elevators, storage sheds—you name it. Most of the time I didn't get their names. I've been thrown out of nightclubs for taking off my clothes on the dance floor. I wanted to have more sex than any other woman in the bar. It was like I lived a double life. I had one set of friends that were classy, and another bunch that did nothing but party. I thought I was hot shit because I could get a man to fuck me. I thought I was in control. Now I'm just a washed-up old whore."

Chastity J. 44
unemployed

"I always have sex on the first date, but I tell myself it's a relationship. Next weekend I'll have a new relationship. Who knows?—maybe I'll get lucky and find the right guy. I think I have a better chance than some bimbo that holds out for the second date. If she waits, he'll be in bed with me. Hell, I probably already did him. The early bird gets the worm—I did *not* just say that!"

Mia D. 33
retail clerk

"I couldn't wait to lose my virginity. I wanted to be sexually active like everybody else, so I'd lie to my friends and tell them I was. I didn't even know what a hymen was for. It's not easy to lose it without your friends finding out. There was this geeky kid in my eighth-grade class with really bad acne, and I decided he was the one. He wasn't cool and none of my friends knew him. After it was done, I was *really* sexually active and no one made fun of me for being a virgin. I even slept with my girlfriend's brother."

Nicole C. 20
thrift store clerk

"We were at our weekly *girl's night out*, bashing men as usual, and the new girl asks 'How *do* you make a man happy?' At least three of us said at the same time 'Learn to swallow!' You should have seen the look on her little baby face. She couldn't speak, but her face said 'Swallow what?' We almost died laughing!"

Theresa G. 34
car wash manager

"If I plan to give a man a blowjob, I make him drink pineapple juice at least an hour before. Sperm tastes awful, but if he drinks the juice it tastes like pineapple. It's a nasty job, but if I don't do it somebody else will. When I figured this out I told my friends, and now they all carry those little pop-top cans of pineapple juice in their purses."

Dena A. 43
grocery clerk

"My blowjob days are over! We've been together so long, if he wants a blowjob he can pay for one in some alley. I just don't want to know about it."

Jody E. 56
insurance agent

"No, really—I have dentures. Top *and* bottom. I had braces for years, but I didn't take care of them. When they took the braces off my teeth just fell apart. I don't take them out for just anybody, but when I do it's under the covers. I won't let anybody see me without them because I look like an old homeless woman. Maybe later if you're not busy—No? Well, maybe another time."

Rhonda W. 41
hairstylist

"I tend bar at a country music nightclub, and we have all the big-name bands. Three of my four cocktail waitresses are married with kids. I shouldn't tell you this, but last weekend—you know Lacey?—she thought the guitar player was hot and she let him know it all night. When the last set was over and the lights came up, he walked past the bar, winked at me, grabbed her hand and took her to his motel room. Her eyes got big, but she followed him like a goddamn puppy. So he's married to a famous singer, and Lacey's husband is at home taking care of their 18-month-old baby. That little bitch called me from the motel room and made me tell her husband she had to stay late. I had to make up some bullshit story for why a cocktail waitress had to stay way past 2:00 AM, and I know he didn't believe me. Lacey quit her job the next day because she and her husband were fighting."

Gail P. 47
bartender

"When I cross the border into Mexico I do things I would never do here. They don't card you, and the bars stay open until 4:00 AM. By that time I'm so shitfaced I can't remember half the stuff I did. One night, I remember standing on the bar with a bunch of other girls, naked from the waist up. My friends told me later I was in a wet T-shirt contest and I ditched my T-shirt. I just remember everybody screaming and clapping. I had the worst hangover for three days. When I woke up I had my pants on, but my really expensive thong was gone. You know what else?—my friends said they were filming me for that show about girls that go wild. If my parents ever find out, there goes my car and tuition. They think I was at a Christian retreat in Tucson."

Mindy K. 19
college student

"I went to the lake for spring break when I was in college. A friend of mine had a boat, and we partied our asses off. I never saw so many people or boats in my life! Everybody was totally wasted and falling in the water and getting arrested. I never knew cops had boats. All I remember is being in a police boat with nothing on but a silver blanket wrapped around me. They charged me with indecent exposure and having sex in public. I wish I knew who I had sex with."
   Rikki C. 27
   social worker

"A really pretty girl loves having sex, not just because it feels good, but because she loves watching someone want her and having his way with her. When the good looks are gone she's useless in bed. She has sex with tons of guys and ends up missing the whole point. I recommend a fat girl or an ugly girl because they appreciate intimacy a lot more."
   Trudy A. 46
   lingerie sales

"I fuck a lot of men, but I prefer men with status, like cops and attorneys—guys that drive nice cars and can afford dinner."
   Hanna M. 29
   middle-school teacher

"My husband and I were very young when we got married, but he had a good job. He supervised the ground crew for a crop-dusting company. Two weeks before our wedding date, he was told that an emergency job had come up for that weekend. I cried and screamed, but he was a supervisor and dedicated to his job. I guess I forgot that his hard work and financial ability had attracted me to him in the first place. *Damn*, I was an immature little bitch! We postponed the wedding for a week, and while he was out-of-town on the job I called my old boyfriend and fucked his brains out the whole weekend. I gave him blowjobs, let him have anal sex with me, and I even cooked for him! In my mind I was getting even for not getting my way. I was so spoiled. I was going to have a honeymoon with or without him, and I did. Oh, my god—I can't believe I did that!"
   Marie M. 28
   waitress

7 SEX

"When I got horny I thought it was sexual frustration, but I was really missing intimacy, and that was my own damn fault. I'd go to a bar and end up in bed with a total stranger, thinking that I was making something better. I'd be ashamed now to count all the guys I had sex with, but all my friends were doing the same thing. I guess that made it okay at the time. Does that mean I'm a whore?"
    Jeannie N. 31
    auto parts delivery

"I just want a fuck-buddy and someone to drink beer with. No commitment."
    Louise R. 47
    ticket sales

"Listen honey—even though I hate men I'd fuck him, married or not, as soon as I'd hug my own kids. There's no line I won't cross to get laid."
    Beth T. 58
    job counselor

"My best friend is getting married next month, and her fiancé is uncomfortable with all the male friends she has. She makes him go to counseling for it, and she and the counselor both have him thinking he's got self-esteem and control issues because he doesn't like it. She goes out to lunch with them every week and her fiancé isn't invited. He's a really sweet man, but he needs a spine transplant. Has she slept with them?—now what the hell do *you* think? *Hell, yes* she's slept with them—still is! She has my spare house key and she uses my guest room like a whorehouse. She just wants to be married for the extra paycheck. If a woman has male friends, she's either slept with them or she's going to sleep with them."
    Karen K. 34
    high-school teacher

"When I was in beauty college I used to give topless haircuts at different guys' homes. One day this old man offered me $100 to cut his hair without my top on, so I did it. I dropped out of school and made lots more money than if I had got my license—it paid for my car."
    Leah J. 27
    topless barber

"I got divorced after twenty-four years of marriage, and my girlfriend talked me into going to a party. It was mostly men, and we had a great time until we woke up the next morning naked, covered with dried god-knows-what, and no memory of what we did. We were putting our clothes on when I noticed something on the bottom of my girlfriend's foot—it was signatures. We both checked our feet, and they had all been autographed! I'd rather not say how many, but it was more than a few."

Barbara B. 60
business owner

"I'm a massage therapist and I work in this ritzy day spa downtown. They do hair and nails, and they have four massage rooms. We have five therapists, and three of us pick up an extra $100 a day by offering 'happy endings' for our male clients. We put a condom on them and it's over in three minutes. It pays a lot better than what the spa pays us. I don't think it's prostitution—I think of it as therapy. I tried prostitution once and I felt dirty after. I was in Las Vegas with some girlfriends, and this old guy gave us $500 apiece to get him off. We spent less than an hour with him so it was good money, but I never did it again."

Shawna T. 39
massage therapist

"I used to spread my legs for any guy who looked at me. Once you start, you get addicted to it. Most of the time it didn't even feel good, but I'd do it again and again. My friends always said 'Guys do it—why can't we?' But not all guys do it. Drunk guys in a bar on Friday night aren't exactly a good sample of what men are like. I was shocked when this one guy asked me out and didn't try to have sex with me. I got aggressive, and he shut me down. I was sitting in an abortion clinic for the fifth time when it hit me that maybe I was ruining my life. Being a whore causes depression."

Patsy Y. 47
home security specialist

"When I have sex with a stranger I imagine what his wife would think if she was watching. It makes me feel powerful. I like being another woman's enemy. It's just a fantasy."

Amy L 28
parking attendant

"When I go to a concert I'm going to fuck somebody important—I mean like in the band! I went to a concert last week and I wanted the lead singer, but I got stuck doing the backup singer. My friend did worse—she fucked the bus driver. She'll do better next time."
Jasmine F. 24
certified nurse assistant

"Oh, don't be shy—I'm already doing all my son's 18-year-old friends. Next time I'll bring some wine coolers to loosen you up."
Kaylyn F. 44
registered nurse

"Why would I want to be with just one man? I have at least five different lovers, and they all think they're the only one. No matter how rich or well-hung a man is, he'll never compete with that. They're dumb and happy, and so am I."
Faith O. 32
photographer

"I always carry Viagra in my purse. I don't have much time for sex, so when I do have it I don't want it to fail. A good all-nighter will get me through the next two weeks."
Jessica H. 26
pharmacy clerk

"I surf the internet for guys with the biggest dicks I can find. Last month I found a monster. I swear it was fifteen inches because we measured it. He dared me to take all of it, and I finally did. Listen, that's nothing—one year I did over 700 guys. I know it sounds impossible, but it's true. I went to the bar every night after work, but I didn't drink. Sometimes I did them in my station wagon in the parking lot. When we finished I'd clean up in the bathroom and grab another one. I didn't drink until I was with the last one, and I'd usually take him home."
Ellen C. 57
state employee

"A 'mercy fuck' is like doing the nerd next door after your date drops you off. It's good karma. It's like giving a homeless guy a few bucks."
Joy M. 23
veterinary receptionist

"Out-of-town sex is the best sex. You don't have to go to Vegas, just a couple of hours away. New faces, new money, and they won't follow you home if you don't tell them where you're from. Save the local guys for when you're ready to get married."

Anya V. 31
medical transcriber

"After the first six months, sex is like an enema. He still loves it, though—*Yuck!* I got married for the big wedding and I love my kids, but I wish his pecker would fall off and then maybe he'd leave me alone."

Erin W. 29
car rental agent

"I had a guy over, so I put my kids to bed early. We had a few glasses of wine and things got crazy. We were on our way upstairs to my bedroom, but we didn't make it. We were stark-ass naked on the stairs and I was sucking him off when I heard *'Mommy?'* Both my boys were at the foot of the stairs wide awake. They were five and seven."

Hanna E. 46
skincare specialist

"Oh, yeah—don't let them fool you. Women will fuck any man in a uniform. My husband was burning leaves in our back yard, and the fire department showed up because it wasn't a *burn day*. One fireman was in the back while my husband hosed down the fire, and the other one was taking my information in the house. I gave him my information, alright. Don't tell my husband!"

Mae R. 34
auto broker

"I got in a big fight with my husband so I decided to fly back home to see my family. I got dressed in my best *'fuck-me'* clothes and stormed out of the house. On the plane, this young soldier in uniform kept making eyes at me. He was just a baby—not much older than my son. It was a big airliner and he was way over on the other side. When I'd had enough, I got up and made my way over to him. I drew him up out of his seat and led him by the hand all the way down the aisle to the restroom. I pulled him inside and started undoing his pants. He started to speak, and I put my finger on his lips and said 'Don't talk.' I gave him the best blowjob ever. I buckled his belt, reapplied my lipstick and took him by the hand back to his seat. You should have seen the faces on the other passengers—they kept pretending to look away. I sat him down, took a magazine from the seat back, put it in his lap and tapped on it with the same finger I had shushed him with. I walked calmly back to my seat, all eyes still on me, sat down and began reading my own magazine. Why did I do it?—I was mad at my husband, for one, and I enjoyed knowing that the young soldier couldn't wait to get back to his base. He'd tell all his buddies what had happened and not a fucking one of them would believe him!"

Prissy T. 37
frequent flyer

"Who the hell started the rumor that men want to have two women at the same time? We're supposed to be independent man-haters, and then we con a girlfriend into having a threesome for some loser guy. We keep attributing *some* men's kinky desires to all the rest of them. And what do we get for it? We just add another twisted memory to the bag of shit in our screwed-up mind. I'm serious—if we hate men so much, why do we do this crazy shit? Have I done it?—I'd rather not say. Okay, I did it once. When I think about it I just want to gag. I was trying to fit in."

Gail A. 43
truck stop manager

"Most of us have tried eating pussy. I had a neighbor who bugged me to have sex with her, and I finally gave in. It was okay, but it wasn't for me. I only did it the one time. It would have been more fun if my boyfriend had been there."

Kari U. 25
clothing sales

"You know what you should do?—I've really thought about this a lot. You should buy a limousine, a folding massage table, and a case of dildos. You could take women on a really cool date in a limo and charge a ton of money for the ride, a massage, and a huge orgasm, and you don't even have to have sex with them! Can you imagine the money you would make? I'll be your first client, and I could be your limo driver too. You'd find a girlfriend that would stay with you for good. Why?—I don't know, she just would."

Felicia S. 29
hardware store clerk

"I can have any man in bed just like that [snapping fingers]. Men are just that way."

Lola Z. 16
student

"Listen, sweetie—the reason we go on about how unfaithful men are is to draw attention away from ourselves. I'll bet if we could miraculously get women to tell the truth, more women are unfaithful than men. We don't do it as often, but we get more out of it. We'll talk about it with each other, but not with men. A man feels guilty after cheating, and thinks his wife will feel like she wasn't taking good care of him. He thinks telling her about it will make it better—big mistake! If you go to a titty bar when you're out-of-town, I'll know because you will tell me. You *have* to tell me—you're a man! But if I go to a club with male strippers, you'll never have a clue. And I'll fuck one of the strippers in the back of my soccer-mom minivan!"

Deborah L. 46
insurance claims adjuster

"Both my ex-husbands are good men, and they both want me back for the kids. I have a child by each of them. I think I'm done partying and sleeping around, but I can't decide which ex to get back together with. I really don't love either one of them—I don't think I've ever been in love. Maybe I should just be a lesbian. What do you think?"

Joni W. 25
elementary schoolteacher

"I don't know why, it just happened. I was happily married for nine years and then I started college. I'm used to men hitting on me, but my anatomy teacher treated me like all the other students. Look at me!—I'm thin and pretty, right? I expected more from him. I flirted with him and made appointments to meet with him in his office, and—nothing! I asked him where he lived and all he would say is that he lived in the southwest part town. I drove around for three weekends looking for his car, and I finally found it. He was shocked when I pulled up in his driveway, but he was very polite. Two weeks later we were in bed. He quit his job and moved away after that."

Rosa H. 34
college dropout

"Oh, grow up! When we fuck somebody else, it's always somebody at work because it's easy and convenient."
Caitlyn T. 47
shipping clerk

"The harder we party, the more guys we sleep with. The more guys we sleep with, the harder we party to forget."
Aurelia B. 32
magazine editor

"New clothes are better than sex. Sex will pay for the clothes, but the clothes are way better. There are only so many different kinds of sex you can have, but new clothing designs come out every season—it's endless!"
Marisa N. 26
investment firm receptionist

"Young man, don't be so ignorant! We're all prostitutes—we all trade sex for something we need or want."
Eleanor Y. 71
retired schoolteacher

8 a fuck-buddy is...

"a guy you're never seen with in public. He knows how to get into your house without being seen."
   Tanya D. 34
   meter reader

"maybe an old boyfriend who's accepted that we'll never be together again, and won't talk about what we do in private."
   Aaralyn Z. 22
   student

"an ugly guy or a fat guy who will act like he doesn't know you if you run into him at the bar—especially if you're with a date!"
   Emmly H. 29
   highway patrol officer

"someone you don't count when you're trying to remember how many men you've had sex with. Don't laugh!—they really *don't* count."
   Willow Y. 34
   auto sales

"you mean *buddies,* don't you—*plural?* I have five of them."
   Kristin P. 27
   office worker

"an ex-husband who drops by for angry sex when my new husband is out-of-town."
Malia A. 25
housewares sales

"who you fuck when you're just not in the mood to curl your hair or put your makeup on. I can be myself around him."
Regina F. 30
photographer

"safe!"
Beatrice K. 36
baker

"just a phone call away when I don't have a real date, or if I don't feel like going out. A fuck-buddy is always on call."
Mindy Q. 20
food server

"someone you call when you're on your period."
Trini H. 29
daycare worker

"the guy who fills in the lonely times between real relationships. He never complains, and he always does his best."
Francesca B. 37
bowling alley manager

"the man with the huge dick who's servicing fifty different women. I've got him on speed-dial."
Eddie C. 52
real estate developer

"the other name for my male friends. They're always there when I need them, and they never interfere with my personal life."
Xandy N. 33
timeshare sales

"a man who will do anything and everything you want, and listen to all your problems because you can't find a decent relationship. They're like a therapist—you can tell them anything, and they don't get mad at you. They have to be gone by morning, though. What would the neighbors think?"
Silvia Y. 44
college professor

"my cousin. *Shit!*—did I really *say* that?"
April V. 46
florist

"always deleted if you have to answer the question 'How many?' When I ask a man how many women he's been with, he always asks me how many men *I've* been with. I hate that!—it makes me lie."
Wynona D. 40
bank teller

"a friend I made a pact with. We agreed that no matter if we're dating, engaged or even married, we will always be there for each other."
McKinsey J. 24
newspaper classified sales

"a pleaser. He'll spend hours making sure you're totally satisfied so you can suffer through the awkwardness of your other relationships. He allows you to refuse sex with the guy you're dating so you can look like a good girl. After the date, you can call your fuck-buddy. Nobody wants to marry a pleaser because eventually you have to please them back, and I just don't have it in me to please anyone but myself."
Courtney T. 24
unemployed

"more convenient than a husband."
Amber L. 47
state employee

"more important than a marriage. Husbands come and go, but a fuck-buddy will always be there for you."
Tabitha G. 31
taxi driver

"a short, bald guy that keeps his mouth shut if he knows what's good for him and wants to get lucky again."
Jade S. 19
between jobs

"a secret lover who keeps you from marrying some guy just because you're horny."
Nedra O. 46
magazine editor

"anybody who buys me enough drinks."
Celina G. 57
restaurant manager

"my girlfriend, because she's really heavy and can't ever get a date. Oh, you mean *men?—Oops!* Well, she's a good fuck-buddy when I don't have a boyfriend."
Aracelly T. 27
clothing sales

"my vibrator with extra batteries. Sex with myself lasts way longer than it does with a man, and I don't feel guilty afterward."
Juanita R. 30
bartender

"the guy I work with that my husband thinks is gay—I told him that so he wouldn't be suspicious. My husband even lets me go 'shopping' with him on Sunday!"
Marla W. 45
aerobics instructor

"an old boyfriend you didn't like in the first place. He's handy though, when you're pissed-off at your husband."
Audrey R. 28
law clerk

"the only person in my life who knows everything about me. He'll be there when I dump my husband. He's like a best friend, but hung like a horse!"
Lorraine L. 34
warehouse clerk

"whoever you want him to be—is that the right answer? My mom always said a man will fuck a rattlesnake if someone holds its head. I'm not hard to look at, so I can have sex with anyone I want. Why do you ask?—do you need a fuck-buddy?"
Jillian K. 25
dental hygienist

"my friend who can't keep a job because he's too busy sleeping around. He's a nice guy, though."
Dericia N. 26
interior designer

"the jerk that gave me herpes!"
   Sophia Q. 57
   painter

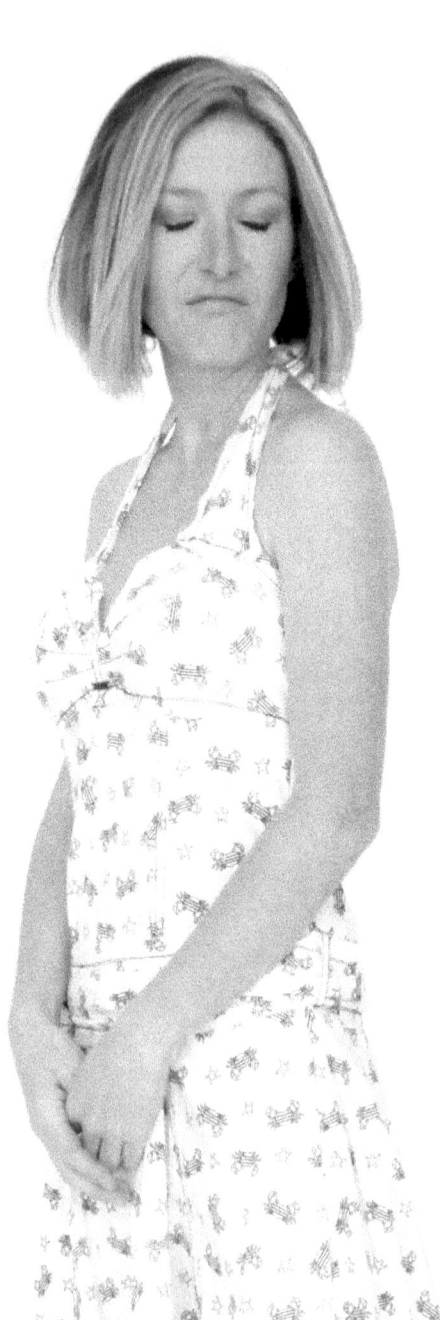

9 damaged goods

"Because of what I've done to myself, I can't be a part of anything successful, relationships or otherwise. There's something inside of me that's punishing me for what I did."
Aubrey J. 29
auto sales

"It's way too late for me. I spent my teens and adult life running wild, and I'm not going to stop now. When a man proposes anything serious, I don't waste time telling him about my past. I used to, but it just made them want to save me. If they don't want to end it I turn into a total bitch until they want to leave. Then I find my next mark, and off we go again!"
Trina E. 36
paint store clerk

"Damaged goods?—it's the old-fashioned way to say a girl fucked herself silly and can't get over it. Back in the old days if a woman lost her virtue, the old women would move her out of town and set her up with an older man who was more understanding and able to appreciate her youthfulness. I think they might have been on to something."
Kitty D. 59
software developer

"We all know how much sex is too much. If we didn't, we wouldn't lie about it. When you catch yourself lying about it, trust me—you've had too much. And then you're not just a whore, you're a liar too! That's makes for a *great* relationship. We're all born with right and wrong—my son isn't even two yet and when he does something wrong, he immediately looks to see if I was watching. We know better."

Sandi J. 29
systems analyst

"I met my husband when I was nineteen, and we got married two years later. The first time we made love I told him I'd only been with one other man. He didn't ask, but for some reason I had to say it. He wasn't surprised or pleased, either one, which confused me. I think I lied so he'd think I was a better person. It didn't bother me during our engagement, but after we got married my lie really started bugging me. All I could think of was what he would do if he knew I'd been with all kinds of men. When I was seventeen I looked twenty-five and I could get into the bars real easy. I didn't have to bring money because men bought me drinks. For two years I woke up in strange beds with guys I didn't even know. I started hating my husband for loving someone who didn't exist—that good girl that was a lie. I felt like he was cheating on me with her. I'd start fights with him for no reason, and I accused him of not even knowing me. I was so horrible to him. I didn't tell him the truth until after our divorce, and he just shook his head. I'll never get married again."

Marcy P. 27
nurse

"I'm a perfect example of what happens to a woman who thought she could have sex with anybody and everybody, and then get over it. When I got older I got tired of the partying and decided I wanted to get married. I played all the games normal husband-hunters play—no bar-hopping, no sex on the first date or in the car, no miniskirts or spike heels. I had perfect hair and nails, watched the news regularly—that kind of bullshit. I dated six men in eight months, and two of them proposed. One of them was an attorney with a beautiful house and not a financial care in the world. The other was a high-school dropout, and he was a carpenter. I married the carpenter. It's been four years and I can't fucking stand him!

He's out-of-work half the time and all he does is watch sports. I wish I'd married the attorney, and for the longest time I couldn't have said why I didn't. I can now, though. I kept replaying a scenario where my past would come up. I didn't want to lie to him —he didn't deserve it. But I didn't want to tell him the truth, either. I guess I didn't mind lying to the husband I chose. My past is totally controlling me, even today. The past will always haunt you. Don't ever forget that."

Cassandra S. 39
legal secretary

"I hate my past. I was totally wild all through my twenties. I can't stop thinking about what I did—it won't go away. I've been married and divorced three times, and I know it's because I'm so screwed-up from the way I behaved. When I'm in a relationship, I'm afraid he's going to hear about all the crazy stuff I did and end it with me. That's all I can think about, so I leave him before he can leave me. If I had it to do over again I would listen to my mom and dad and go to college. I'm tired of lying about my past."

Heather W. 35
insurance company receptionist

"All the women I work with know what I was—a whore. How?—they can just tell. There's something about a woman with a past that other women just pick up on. When their husbands come to the office, they keep them away from me. It's so obvious. The only way I could be happy in a relationship is if I was a virgin again. If I was, I'd wait until I was married."

Allison T. 33
office worker

"The worst part about sleeping with more men than I can count is that it doesn't even feel good anymore. I always thought if I found the right guy it would be 'making love.' All I ever did was fuck. It feels like doing the dishes—I can't wait to get it done. I try to fantasize about someone else when I'm doing it, but that doesn't work anymore. Every time I have sex it's always with a different guy, and I try to convince myself that it's going to be a relationship, but I know better. I should have charged for it from the beginning—I'd be a millionaire by now. Maybe I should just stop having sex."

Katrina H. 44
living off my parents

"When I was young, I thought I was *it!* I could crook my finger and have anyone I wanted. My finger is still sore! I'd spend all day at work, and half the night on a barstool or in the back seat of some guy's car. The bouncer used to write my name on a napkin and tape it to my barstool. I was the only one there with a reservation. I never thought it would ruin my future. I just knew one day I would meet a young doctor like Doogie Houser, take a long, hot shower and walk down the aisle in a white dress. Instead, I'm useless to a man. I'm spoiled rotten and nobody can give me the attention I need. At my age, I look stupid sitting on a barstool—my ass is too wide. There's a picture, huh?"

Prudence B. 45

caterer

"Bi-curious is bullshit! Bi-curious is when you've fucked every single man in town, and half the married ones. Other women point at you and pull their husbands and kids closer when they see you. A whore who claims to be bi-curious has already destroyed herself, and can't find anyone to get naked with. My sister is a lesbian, and I mean an honest-to-god, from-birth lesbian. She's not curious—she's certain. She's had her heart broken over and over by these skanky little bitches who are pretending. My sister doesn't want to have wild sex with just anyone. She wants a real relationship, not some whore who ran out of men to fuck. They're worse than any loser guy I ever dated. I hate them—I'm sorry, but I do."

Estelle U. 41

resort management

"I can't stand to listen to women who brag about sleeping with every man who smiles at them. And then they bash men because they can't find a meaningful relationship. I just want to puke! They should have listened better in Sunday school. They act like a man is obligated to marry them regardless of their past."

Jessi I. 24

long-term caregiver

"Listen to me, now—I was a promiscuous young woman—*very* promiscuous! I knew it all, and nobody could tell me otherwise. I learned the hard way how women and cars are alike—low mileage is preferable. Not only to men, but to your friends as well. What woman wants to introduce her husband to a friend with a

reputation? Abandoning morality has its price, and I've been paying it for years. The price is solitude, before you even reach old age."
Harriet V. 68
laundromat attendant

"These women sleep around for years and they end up being defined by their genitals and their ability to get lucky at a bar. If they think it won't follow them forever, they're crazy. They think they're not hurting anyone but themselves, but when they start having children instead of abortions, how well-adjusted will they be as mothers? I promise you—not very."
Sylvia F. 41
teen mental-health counselor

"Every time I fuck somebody new, I lose a big chunk of myself. Now there's nothing left of me. Why do I keep doing it over and over? I think I need to quit hanging around my friends. They're all whores, and when I'm with them it seems okay to be one too."
Reyna W. 26
retail clerk

"I didn't even think about it back then. I just had sex whenever I felt like it. The only regret I have is not being a *true* blonde anymore. I must have scorched it on that football team."
Margie R. 59
short-order cook

"I finally realized I was a slut and I knew if I wanted to settle down with a man, he'd have a problem with my past. So when I was done whoring around I decided to move away and lie about it. It turns out that men have less trouble with my past than I do. It's a whore who has trouble being in a relationship, not the man she's with. I hate myself. It makes me sad that I gave away my virginity so easily. I wish I had thought of it sooner."
Temple S. 32
retail sales

"When I was a virgin my friends made fun of me, and they all said that the past doesn't matter anymore. They said guys do it all the time, so we should too. Guess what?—the past *does* matter, and I wish I'd never done it."
Cynthia J. 17
student

"Once you give a few drunken blowjobs to strangers in the men's room, you're pretty much toast. If you do get married, you know exactly what you'll tell your husband when you give him his honeymoon blowjob—'I'm not really very good at this.' We're all lying bitches! When I woke up in the bed of my friend's pickup with dried cum in my hair and a really sore throat, I decided that I probably wasn't meant to be a wife or mother."

Megan A. 48
911 dispatcher

"Don't get me wrong, now—there's nothing wrong with interracial relationships. But when white women who've destroyed themselves with immoral behavior regard a black man as their last hope for a relationship, I'm incensed! And it's not just blacks they turn to, but also Latino men. If they think skin color reflects a man's tolerance for immorality in a woman, they are sorely mistaken. I've heard white girls talking about their wide rear ends, and how black men find them irresistible. This kind of talk is the epitome of racial ignorance. There are unsavory people of all races, and these ignorant girls will surely find the worst of them."

Cloris D. 55
retired military (African-American)

"Women hate it, but it's true—we're different from men when it comes to sex. A man can sleep with an entire girl's volleyball team on Friday, meet the girl of his dreams on Sunday, and treat her like a queen for the rest of her life. A woman, on the other hand, will use her past as an excuse to torture a man for not knowing just how bad she really was. She never forgets her past, and thinks about it day and night. Women who think they can do *everything* a man can do are delusional."

Faith M. 49
driving instructor

"My brother got tired of being devoured by American women. He went to Thailand for the summer and met the most wonderful woman ever. She treats him like gold, and he takes such good care of her, too. It's beautiful to watch. You know what's funny, though?—my husband and I know a lot of other couples and they all know my new sister-in-law. The men love her and are delighted for my brother. But the women?—they hate her! The idea of it makes them furious. They don't even know exactly what it is they hate, but I know—they're all damaged and they believe men should suffer for it. I was on the fence at first, until I saw how happy my brother is. Since she came into our lives, I find myself treating my husband a little better. She's a good influence."

Nellie P. 44
golf pro

"I *know* what's wrong with me—I'm just an overweight, worn-out old whore. It kills any plans I try to make, or relationships I might get into. I can't believe in anything anymore, and I get really mad if a man shows me a little attention. I think 'You stupid bastard—if you only knew.' I hate men because of something they don't even know about me, and I blame them for not knowing."

Cherry G. 49
bus driver

"Who cares how many men I slept with? I got engaged to this guy from a rich family, and I told him I couldn't have sex with him because I was a virgin. My parents paid for the surgery, and presto!—I'm a virgin again. It's called a hymenoplasty. Lots of women are having it done. They use microsurgery to rebuild your hymen. There was an older woman in the waiting room who was doing it for her husband for their twentieth anniversary. You don't even have to lie about your past. The nurse told me to say 'I'm a virgin'—not 'I'm *still* a virgin,' and then it's not a lie. We didn't get married because I still wanted to party with my friends, and he caught me a bunch of times getting really drunk at the bar. He said I didn't act like a virgin—*Duh!*"

Abby R. 24
still living with parents

"It's true—it depends not only on the quantity of sex, but how debased and vulgar it was. I've tried to live down my past, but I never will. Whores will either still be doing it at eighty, or something will snap and they'll avoid it completely. I snapped out of it, but it didn't mean I had to be lonely. I married a paraplegic in a wheelchair. He can't have sex, but we share more intimacy than any hundred men I've been with."

Estelle C. 62
retired

"You bet too much sex is bad for you. Hell, sweetie—I was forty years old before I knew that the pillow goes under your *head*. I haven't had a stiff neck since!"
    Marilyn O. 74
    retired court clerk

"Lying to your husband about your past makes you insane. I tried it with three different husbands. I finally figured it wasn't their fault—it was mine. You have this big dirty secret that's trying to bust out, but you're committed to your lie. It gets really stressful and after a while you start acting out. You can actually feel yourself going crazy. My advice is to get a handle on it before you start lying about it. Trust me—the past *does* matter."
    Berta Y. 36
    mental patient (just kidding)

"If a woman finds a decent man and she lies to him about her sexual past, she will ruin the relationship. The first symptom will be jealousy, even if she's never been jealous before. If she starts feeling jealous it's proof that she has finally found a man worth keeping. Trouble is, *she's not* and she knows it. I've seen it a hundred times. It's that simple and easy to predict."
    Emma Q. 53
    wedding planner

"Men don't have a clue how ripped-up and damaged these women are. They offer themselves up to be destroyed, and all the next man gets is a trainload of baggage and the lies she tells to cover it up."
    Dorothy F. 56
    district court judge

"You know you're damaged goods when you're at a party with your husband, and you see the guy you fucked on the bar in front of everyone at a wild party two years ago. So you go to the bathroom to hide and throw up. Been there, done that."
    Pam A. 31
    sous-chef

10 penis size

"Women trade penis stories like baseball cards! A penis is just one more thing that belongs to a man that women want. Why can't we be happy with what we've got? If they start doing penis transplants, half my girlfriends would go get the biggest one they had."
Leigh M. 40
banquet hostess

"Listening to women at work talk about them is like listening to my sixth-grader and his friends comparing skateboards. I shudder to think that these women are populating the earth. They talk like they actually *have* a penis. A lot of women claim to hate men, but can't seem to get them off their minds—and for the most ridiculous reasons. He's so well-endowed, and you're the *only* one he's sleeping with, right? Can he earn a living? Will he take care of you when you're sick?"
Juliet A. 46
office manager

"A big cock is great for a one-night stand and to impress your friends, but I wouldn't want to marry a man with a big one. Big ones are for fucking, regular-sized ones are better for making love."
Franny D. 27
physician's assistant

"I work with a lot of men and women, and the women talk about sex way more than the men do. It's usually about who has the biggest dick on our staff. If it's that great, one of them is shooting herself in the foot by bragging about it. The others will be all over him and he'll think he's a god."

Georgia T. 48
warehouse worker

"Women who shop for bigger penises are uneducated whores who (1) don't know the first thing about making love and will try to fuck your husband, or (2) had kids, ate everything in sight when they were pregnant, and now you could park a truck in their vajayjay! They know who they are."

Louisa L. 43
registered nurse, women's health clinic

"The best lovers don't need a penis of any particular size, just the desire to please someone other than themselves. All these bed-hopping women don't have a clue what a good lover is. He's a person who does everything to the best of his ability, and not just in bed. A good man with an average-sized penis can make your body do things you never imagined possible."

Hillary V. 34
web designer

"Oh, my god! I visit my mother every day at a short-term care facility, and last week a nurse stopped me outside her room to sign some paperwork. I could hear my mom laughing with two other ladies, and they were talking about how well-hung a male resident is. I guess he put his gown on with the opening in the front. The nurse giggled and left, but I was too embarrassed to go in the room! I thought I'd wait until the gossip stopped, but they kept going on and on! I finally left and called my mother from home. She's seventy-eight!—is nothing sacred?"

Jerry U. 47
county health department

"You know, there's big enough, and then there's way *too* big. I was just out of high school when I got married. We waited to have sex until our wedding night, and nothing ended up happening. It was a year before he was able to penetrate me, and it always hurt like crazy. We fought about it all the time and we finally divorced. The walls of my vagina are torn and I have really bad scar tissue now. Every time I hear these girls brag about how big some guy is, I get sick. If that's all they're looking for in a man and the word gets out, they're in for a big disappointment."

Susan K. 28
hospital worker

"I spent thirteen years with a man who was *very* well-hung, but I never had a vaginal orgasm—it hurt too much. The only way he could make me climax was orally."

Tiffany R. 34
trust fund brat

"I went out with my girlfriend's cousin and we ended up parking to have a little fun. When he whipped that thing out, I almost died. The head of it was the size of a coffee cup and God only knows how long it was. He acted pleased with himself. I made him take me home before somebody got hurt!"

Quinque I. 24
college student

"That's all my girlfriends talked about—big dicks. I had a chance to date a black man, so I jumped on it. My girlfriends warned me to brace myself because he might kill me with it. When he took off his pants, I must have looked really disappointed. He pulled his pants back up and told me that it happened all the time. He was smaller than my old boyfriend. I felt really bad and I apologized, but he never called again."

Lorna E. 36
college student

"A vagina was designed to handle everything from a tampon to a baby. If a woman needs a huge penis to get off, she's the one with the problem—not her man."

Patricia W. 66
retired truck driver

"The best way to fuck with a guy's mind is, when he asks you if it was good, just say 'I've seen *smaller* ones.' I say it all the time to get a reaction and to make them try harder next time."

Alisa G. 25
secretary

"Women always seem to overdo it. They get these unnaturally large breast implants, and then they scold men for looking at them. Women hate men who like big boobs, but just listen to them go on about a big dick. What a bunch of hypocrites!"

Adriana H. 31
security guard

"Having a boyfriend with a big cock is kind of like having one who's a bodybuilder—everyone wants to try him on. The best way to handle it is to treat him really good and always be there for him, and most of all don't tell your friends! There is no such thing as a woman friend. Your best friend will be the first one in line telling him that you're banging a guy at work just so she can get in his pants. Now I'm getting all worked-up because it happened to me. Friends suck!"

Lane G. 34
media sales

"You can't climax if it hurts like hell. All this talk about penis size just makes men feel inadequate—it's hateful. My ex was well-hung, but he had to be really careful or he'd hurt me. It wasn't fun, it was stressful. Women are just screwing themselves because a man who believes he's not adequate won't call you again, and he damn sure won't spend much for dinner."

Kora C. 54
tax consultant

"Holy shit, it really hurts! I feel sorry for him because he can't get too excited and be himself, or he'll tear me open. It's a real problem because we're always stressed-out about it. I told him he should be a porn star—he didn't think it was funny. It's like he has a disability."

Deena P. 34
cosmetologist

"A huge penis is a nuisance. I'd much rather be with an average-sized man with a job and a future than an unemployed horndog that hangs out at bars to service the young girls. There might be a few well-endowed men who love their wives, but not many. My husband had this problem—actually it was *my* problem. I couldn't keep women away from him on the internet, and the girls from work would actually come knocking on our door on weekends looking for him. He finally got fired for fraternization. Girls are worse now than men ever were. If a man has a credit card or a big bulge, it's like going to the dog pound with a pork chop hung around his neck. We're divorced now."

Delilah R. 52
emergency medical technician

"These women think they aren't getting bedded properly if a man doesn't have twelve inches. You know why a woman thinks her husband's penis is shrinking?—because she gets fat, has three kids, and her only exercise is opening the freezer to get more ice cream. Her fuzzy toy gets lazy and turns into a flabby abyss that could swallow a man. She *could* do exercises to make it tighter, but that's about as likely as going on a diet. I'm sorry, but these lazy pigs spend hundreds of dollars on a plus-size spandex wardrobe, enroll in my course, and after the first class I never see them again. I did see a group of them at a nightclub wearing their spandex with lacy tops and spike heels—picture that for a minute! Men's penises are just fine, and always have been. 'Kegel'—it's the exercise that makes it tighter."

Vivian K. 38
physical therapist/aerobics instructor

"It's over-the-top crazy! Women are bragging about a body part they'll never have—it's like name-dropping. Who gives a shit who you know? If she thinks a big dick is a trophy, she's never had a good lover. Couples need time to learn about each other before they can be good lovers. These sorry little bimbos get drunk, go home with someone they just met, and come in the next week complaining about the sex. If I were a man, the last person I'd expect to satisfy is a drunken, inexperienced little slut. But they always blame the man."

Delaney B. 39
bartender

"A young woman doesn't know that when she goes through menopause, her vagina shrinks back to smaller that it was in her teens. I'm as tight now as I ever was when I was a girl. Young women who think they need a big man will be grateful for an average-sized penis after a while."

Kate F. 64
elementary-school principal

"I need a man with a big one to satisfy me. After having a baby, I'm so big most men would fall in. I'm a big girl and I need a big man to find my happy place."

Jeanette Q. 27
car rental service

"These women looking for big penises expose themselves as the shallowest of humanity. If a man focused merely on a physical attribute that I happen to possess, I wouldn't cross the street for him. Women invented terms like *'ass man'* and *'leg man'*, which do nothing but belittle men. Modern women are so pitiful. They have objectified men to a far greater degree than they ever were by the men. Guys may not be as complicated as we are, but valuing a man's individuality is apparently too much work for most of us. It's easier to judge them as a group and avoid the effort. Women are the laziest members of society now, and I'm almost sorry to be one."

Betty Y. 53
college administrator

"You have to tell him about the guy you had before with the big thing. There are ways to bring it up that make it look like it was his idea. He needs to think you always have other choices, in case he doesn't treat you right. If he thinks he's smaller than the last guy, he'll spend more money on you to make up for it. Sooner or later we have to bring it up."

Tawney I. 19
unemployed

"My nephew has quite the gift in that department. We made fun of him since he was little, and I think we gave him a complex about it. He's very smart and handsome, but he can't keep a girlfriend because they always want to know what other girls thought of his gift. He doesn't want to talk about the other girls. I told him to lie and say that he's a virgin!"

Taylor P. 49
housewife

"Women have made such a big deal about black men and penis size, I can't get a date anymore! White men are so intimidated by our obsession with size that when a guy who's interested in me learns I was married to a black man, they run like hell. The first time it happened I thought it was racist. Then I had a date who told me honestly that because he hears all these women bragging about penis size, he knew he couldn't satisfy me after I'd been with a black man. I asked how many black ones he'd seen, and he admitted it wasn't many, but he'd often overheard women talking about it. He never called after that."

Hailey V. 44
city clerk

"I hate a big penis! My vagina is so tight, I lost two husbands because of it! My gynecologist has to use a child's speculum to do my pap smear, and both my children had to be delivered by cesarean section. My new boyfriend loves it because he doesn't need a huge penis to please me. Everything is relative, I guess."

Chanel N. 48
waitress

"When you're complaining about your ex to a new guy, tell them he was so big he hurt you. It really fucks up their brain. What are they going to think?—'I'm so happy to be smaller than him?' I think every guy secretly wants to hurt a woman down there."

Marti H. 32
r.v. sales

11 man-haters

"We're man-haters because we're told to be. It's popular, and our friends expect us to hate men. Wow! I know what you're thinking—what else would we do if we were told to? I don't really hate men, I just act like I do."
McKinley W. 20
customer service representative

"We can't make up our minds—do we hate men, or do we want one? If we want a *good* man we have to do something to please him, and we don't know how. Men scare me because I hear so much about what they want, and I don't know how to do it. And anyway, what's wrong with making a man happy? If I knew how, I would. Maybe I should just tell my man-hating girlfriends to go fuck themselves and quit telling me what to think."
Tish R. 26
coffee shop manager

"Why do we hate men? We hate them to satisfy our friends. Even a prostitute knows that if you please a man, he'll knock himself out to please you back. We have some serious problems, don't we? And no, I'm not a prostitute—yet."
Jesi T. 31
theater manager

"We don't just hate *men*—we hate women who have a good man. We get so fucking paranoid if a woman we know finds a nice guy. If she looks happy with her new boyfriend, we hit her with a list of questions that'll make her have doubts—*'Oh, so he has money?—he's probably a drug dealer. Oh, he's divorced?—you better run a background check because he probably beat his ex-wife—better yet, call her and get the truth'.* Women can be anyone's worst nightmare if we join forces."

Star V. 31
fashion retail

"I know we blame men for everything wrong with our lives. We don't give credit to the men who are doing everything right, either. We'd rather doubt their intentions so we don't have to face the possibility that we missed out on something."

Heather W. 43
private tutor

"I especially hate an accomplished or really good-looking man. They're just too much work—go to the gym, look your best, be nice all the time. It would take way too much to deserve him. Before I got fat I dated a lot of men like that and it wore me out. They're too perfect. They didn't make demands, but I could just see myself with one of them looking like I do now. That's why I have a fat slob with a beer and the TV remote on the couch—it's easier."

Karol I. 47
daycare

"I remember exactly when I decided to be a man-hater. My old boss was a genuine asshole and he treated everybody like dogs. I wanted to tell him off, but I couldn't afford to lose my job so I kept it all inside. I really hated him and I blamed the way he was on his gender. Before I knew it all men pissed me off, and I *liked* being called a man-hater. I even raised my daughter to hate men. I think I really messed up her life."

Lillian T. 54
shipping broker

"Women hate men because men still know how to have fun. When most women think of fun, they immediately think of a man. It's easier to have fun with a man than by yourself or with your twisted girlfriends. I even hated my ex-husband because he knew how to

have fun with our kids. I divorced him and moved away with the kids. It was childish, I know, but I wasn't going to let my kids want him more than they did me."
   Adonna F. 49
   janitor

"Man-hating is worse when we all get together. It's like we're soldiers against men. We can't stand each other as a rule, but when one of us has something bad to say about a man, we're like sharks. I think we need support from other women to keep us thinking we're right about men. What if we all found out we were wrong about them?—I don't even want to think about that."
   Carolina S. 28
   temp service

"Women are total idiots! If you want them to completely change their thinking, all you need is a new reality show and four commercials with taglines. At least a fourth of the female viewers will change immediately, and they'll make the taglines part of their vocabulary. Then they'll verbally influence the rest to change. The media exploits our hatred for men. We don't call them a *'target'* group for nothing."
   Lydia V. 42
   advertising consultant

"I hated my ex-husband because he was so damn good-looking and he didn't do a goddamn thing to be that way. Maybe I hated his metabolism. I weighed 120 pounds in my wedding dress—now look at me! The fatter I got, the more I suspected him of sleeping around. I hated women who looked like me when I got married. Maybe I should hate food. Maybe I hate myself. Maybe you should just shut the fuck up before I start hating *you* too!"
   Janet U. 46
   travel agent

"I raised my daughter to hate men and exploit them until her looks are gone. I made her watch videos from strip clubs so she would have an advantage in the real world. I'll be proud of her if she starts stripping. Men are pigs, and I don't want her on welfare and food stamps because some lazy asshole won't work."
   Roberta M. 36
   warehouse manager

"I especially hated men when I needed the oil changed in my car. I had to be nice to a man to get it done, and they wanted me to *stay* nice after it was done. So like a good man-hater, I bought a book, some oil, and a filter so I didn't have to ever be nice again. I cross-threaded the drain plug, all my oil leaked out, and I blew up my engine. I went back to being nice every three thousand miles."

Sis J. 38
self-employed

"We hate men because we're raging hypocrites! We're supposed to be able to eliminate them from our lives, and if we don't we get in trouble with our friends. If we truly hated men we'd have to stop supporting them by buying new breasts and having our cars fixed. We can't hate them completely, so it's never complete. It's a job that never gets done, and it's exhausting."

Deborah R. 36
exotic dancer

"Women are so fucking desperate to find a man, even though they claim to hate them. You should hear what they say in groups—*'I want a guy to love me the way I am—All the good ones are taken, aren't they?—I just want a man who makes me laugh'*. I hear this bullshit all day long at work from the laziest and fattest women who would have a seizure if they accidentally had an intelligent thought."

Gail D. 46
secretary

"This man-hater movement has made our country a house divided. There are only two sexes in this country, for the most part, and one of them regards the other as their enemy. It's a cold civil war—not too bright if you ask me."

Edmona Y. 57
university administrator

"Man-haters don't just make themselves miserable, they fucking recruit like Jim Jones or David Koresh! I almost lost my husband because of the influence of other women at work. When I realized that I was going home already mad at my husband just because he's a man, it was almost too late. It took me six months to apologize to him for a year of my bitching for no reason. I mean it—I almost lost my marriage! When he finally forgave me he confided that he'd

been saving money to move away. I transferred to another branch and I now I don't socialize with any of the women at work. They think I'm a snob or in an abusive relationship, and they actually think my husband won't let me go out with them. They have no idea that they are poison to a good relationship."
Kinley I. 31
bank teller

"Women hate men and don't even know why! They call them *assholes* and *boys with toys*, they run them into the ground and they don't know why they're doing it. They're having sex with other women and they're not even lesbians! They act like they know something about men, when all they really know about are the losers they pick up at the bars."
Shannon E. 48
receptionist

"The more educated a woman becomes, the more she hates men because she realizes that no matter how independent she is, a man will always have accomplished more, and with less effort. She knows he'll be her boss."
Darcy C. 38
college admissions

"An accurate predictor of what a woman is really up to is how much she claims to hate men. The more she hates them, the more men she has sex with. She doesn't hate men—she hates herself."
Beta N. 67
retired

"It's the parents of these adolescent bimbos who started man-hating. They pay for a wedding that she doesn't deserve, and then they feel needed when she asks for more money to make ends meet, which causes them to think less of her husband. Every time she needs more money they blame her husband for not being a good provider. She picks up on their insistence that he's worthless, and starts agreeing with them to get sympathy and more money. Think about it—if you want free money, you have to get sympathy first. Her parents enable her to continue living beyond her means, the marriage ends, and it's the man's fault! Complicated, huh?"
Melody S. 34
restaurant supplier

"Men fight wars to protect our freedom and our safety, and now *we've* become the enemy! How do you fight that? Women even wear T-shirts that explain just how much they hate men. My son will be looking for a wife in a couple of years, and I'm terrified about what he might drag home. I'm seriously thinking about finding him a woman from another country where they still know the value of a good man."

Nicola S. 36
cake decorator

"I hate men because not one of them has bought me a house or a new car. I told every one of them 'I like money—lots of it!' I've slept with most of them, so I know what I'm talking about."

Terina U. 38
between careers

"I teach four-day management seminars for major companies. I've been everywhere in the country from coast to coast, and it never fails—get a group of women together and the first thing they have in common is hating men. The next thing is partying and getting laid while the kids are with the husband for four days. I feel fortunate to have a wonderful husband, but I know better than to talk about it. The attendees are women of all ages, but none of them are as mature as my 13-year-old daughter, and they act like animals."

Kimberley Y. 47
management consultant

"I spent twenty years being alone and hating men because I was raped. I blamed all men for the actions of one. When I found a good man, I had to get rid of my friends because they called me a traitor. They did everything they could to break us up. One of my *'friends'* invited my guy to come to her house to help her with her car while her husband was out-of-town. She told him to come alone, and she did it right in front of me! She said she wanted to show me that he was a pig like all men. He told her he didn't want to be away from me that long, and to just drop off her car and he'd fix it when he had time. She got really pissed-off, and accused me of being brainwashed and controlled by him."

Jolene C. 44
private caregiver

"Women hate men because they can do more than women. Men and women can each do some things better than the other. The difference now is, women don't do what they are best at—they quit. Women are trying to be like the men and compete with them. Every day is a failure for most women. They work too hard and earn too little, and they get tired and mean. Men haven't changed—they still do what they've always done. It's American women who have changed."

Sita G. 48
business owner

"After I got married I put on weight. After my baby was born, I put on more weight. When I saw skinny women I put on weight! The fatter I got, the more I hated my husband because he still looked like our wedding photos, and he never said a word about my weight. Everybody treated me like a handicapped pig—like I didn't know I was fat. When family came over, they sat on the floor and put their kids on their laps so nobody would sit on my loveseat, because it was the only place I would fit. I was full of hate, and my husband didn't do anything to deserve it. When I came to my senses I lost 132 pounds, and my husband still loves me. Hating men is just a cover-up for hating yourself."

Norma P. 38
housewife

"I used to be beautiful, but the fatter I got, the more I hated him for being with me. If he left me for being fat it would mean that he kept his high standards. That's one of the things that attracted me to him. If he's with a fat pig he obviously has no standards, and then I'm with a man who has no standards. I hate him because he lowered them to stay with me, when I'm a fat pig."

Tammy M. 51
unemployed

"I'm sick of my friends trying to recruit me into their man-hater cult. My husband is a terrific person, and they hate it. They treat their men like crap and then wonder why they're hard to get along with. They need to start hating their own actions."

Sharon L. 51
lab technician

"This collective hatred for men is not based on experience or on women's own designs. They've been lured into a mob of man-haters for a purpose so complex that when I've tried to explain it to them, I just get a blank stare."

Gilda F. 47
therapist

"We *have* to hate men because that's who we blame everything on. If we just blame them without hating them too, we feel guilty about it. I thought I was over it until I ran into a friend of my ex-husband's ten years after our divorce. I hadn't seen or heard from my ex in all those years, but I couldn't shut my mouth about how it was his fault and not mine. Actually, the divorce was really my fault. I went from 140 pounds to 280 in the first two years of our marriage, and all I did was sleep and eat. I'm sorry now."

Jackie L. 61
home improvement

"All you have to do is say the words 'ex-husband' or 'ex-boyfriend,' and women start lighting torches and forming a vigilante group. Hating men is contagious."

Daphne B. 45
attorney

"When we got divorced my ex-husband threatened to fight for custody of our daughter, so I accused him of molesting her and that was the end of that. I had the detective and the district attorney eating out of my hand. I didn't mean for it to go that far, but what was I supposed to do?—tell them I was lying? He did seven and a half years in prison. Everything you need to know about how to do it is on the internet. Hey, I did what I had to do."

Rayla E. 32
highway construction flagger

"My first husband was a high-school dropout and he worked on a farm—then he decides to go to school. I thought 'Yeah, right.' He could hardly spell his own name, and his handwriting sucked. First he took night classes to get his G.E.D. and he did really good. Then the dipshit wants to start college. We did a budget and I acted like I was all for it—*acted*, mind you. In his first semester he got a scholarship for good grades! I thought 'Ohhh, no—I'm not gonna

be married to some smart-ass with a college degree. So I stopped taking the pill and I got pregnant. So much for college."
Darlene H. 33
housewife

"I hate men because I know they'd rather have a gorgeous babe like on TV. I can't blame them—some of them are so perfect-looking I'd do them myself. I know that if a man wants me, he's settling."
Charla D. 49
fair vendor

"My best friend got married and she was totally happy for two years, and then she moved back home with her parents. It shocked everybody. She told us all how he beat her the whole time. I used to run with a bad crowd, and she asked what it would take to have him killed—and I actually considered it! But get this—four years later I went to work for him, and I'll tell you what—he's nothing like the man she described at all. He is the kindest, most generous guy I've ever met. And he's good in bed, too."
Olive G. 38
law firm receptionist

"You know where you can find most man-haters?—*With a man!*"
Saasha T. 27
clothing wholesaler

12 lies

"Lying is *not* a sin—it's an art form. If you're good at it you can get things you really don't deserve, and avoid the nasty consequences you *do* deserve."
Karen B. 43
housewife

"Men suck at lying. You have to do it a lot to get good at it, and women have had much more practice. Men would get into less trouble if they could just learn to hide the truth better."
Jade K. 23
truck stop attendant

"If I lie to my boyfriend and he believes me, I don't trust him. You should never trust a man who believes your lies. He probably knows I'm lying and he's just not saying anything. He'll use it as a reason to lie to me."
Victoria E . 23
shopping cart attendant

"If you want to know what your new girlfriend looks like when she's lying, just ask her how many men she's had sex with. Watch closely, and don't forget the look on her face. Trust me—she'll lie."
Lorna H. 28
bookkeeper

"What am I supposed to do?—tell my husband his sister and I got drunk and danced naked at the beach in Mexico? I don't think so! Anyway, that was two years ago."
    Vidi G. 25
    shoe sales

"My brother-in-law was drinking coffee with his friends at the tire store when he heard some guy bragging about 'fucking' my sister. He walked over to get in on the conversation, and got introduced around. The guy that was doing my sister got jumpy and asked my brother-in-law if he knew her. He said he didn't, and the guy was relieved to hear it. When he got home he asked my sister if she'd been having an affair and she completely denied it, until he told her that he'd just had coffee with the dirtbag. I had known about it for a long time, but I never said anything. I'm glad my brother-in-law never asked me about it. I would have lied too."
    Lawanda D. 42
    retail clerk

"The best lies always have a little truth in them for believability. I have to admit, I'm a really good liar. If my husband walked in on me and caught me in bed with two of his best friends, I could get him to doubt what he saw."
    Charlene W. 27
    produce manager

"Women have to lie if we're trying to compete with men. They'll always kick our asses when it comes to determination and stamina. The closer we get to winning the war against men, the more exhausted we are. And if we ever did win that stupid imaginary war, it would be a hollow victory."
    Lorena V. 41
    information tech

"I thought I was a good liar, but my husband was smarter than I thought. We got in a fight, and I packed my stuff and left for a week. When I came home I said I'd been at my sister's house. He called her, and our stories didn't match. So I told him I'd checked into a motel for the week to rest and get my thoughts together, and I'd lied about it because I didn't want to answer a bunch of questions. He acted like he believed me until later that night when he asked me for the receipt from the motel. I dug through my suitcase and bags, pretending to look for the receipt. I swore to him I'd been at the motel. He called them up and the manager said he could get a copy of the receipt, no problem. Then he handed me my jacket and said 'Let's go get your receipt.' I was busted—I was really at my ex-husband's house the whole time."

Catarina A. 43
dental receptionist

"If a man doesn't ask me how many guys I've slept with, I get nervous. You want a man to think you're a good girl, and I tell them I've only been with two other guys. If he hasn't asked by the second week, I can't help it and I bring it up. It usually works, but my last boyfriend didn't fall for it. He said 'If you offer a man a body count when he didn't ask for it, you're lying.' I won't do that again!"

Calista Y. 25
retail associate

"If I get caught in a big fat lie, I'll just point the finger at a man. I can make up stories about a man that will make everyone suspect him instead of me. Besides, I'm pretty and everybody believes pretty. He's a man and men are pigs!"

Ellie C. 24
unemployed

"The problem with lying is, if he believes you he looks stupid. I lie to my husband all the time and I hate it when he believes me. Why doesn't he check out some of this shit and catch me at it? I'd respect him more if he did. Then I'd probably be mad at him for not trusting me. Men are screwed either way."

Lainie J. 27
copy center clerk

"I don't have to lie—it's just more fun to always be in control."

Crystal A. 45
fast-food worker

"I like it when people believe me. Lies are so fantastic—at least mine are. Telling lies keeps people interested, because the truth is boring."

Gina P. 28
auto parts delivery

"It's perfectly natural to lie to a man. It's instinctive for a woman to deceive. It tests our power and control."
Josie W. 39
pharmacist

"A person needs to be extremely careful out there because everyone lies about their sexual history. You would not believe how many decent people I treat for HIV and hepatitis who were lied to by partners who knew they were infected."
Pazi K. 47
medical doctor

"There are lies you tell to men, then there are lies you tell *about* men. You tell men lies to get what you want from them. You tell lies *about* them to get even, and make bad things to happen to them—like lying to the police, or in a courtroom."
Lakota W. 26
looking for work

"If a man was smart he would make his fiancée take a polygraph test before getting married. Or better yet, get to know her friends really well. If a woman is lying to him, one of her friends will crack and tell him."
Vel W. 24
party planner

"If you're a whore, you lie about stuff to get a man to think what you want him to think. It's the only power we have."
Lauren S. 43
animal control officer

"Oh, we'll lie about partying, drinking, fucking, and how much money we spent—you name it."
Rosanna O. 47
storefront designer

"I got married and divorced when I was really young, and when my ex found a new girlfriend it really pissed me off. Old story—I didn't want him, but I didn't want anyone else to have him either. I went with my brother to a dance after the rodeo, and I got drunk and fucked the drummer in the band. I was pretty back then and I could have any man I wanted. I forgot about it until I missed my period. I was knocked-up like some cheap groupie by a goddamn drummer,

but I told everybody it was my ex-husband's baby. His new girlfriend was ditzy, but she did the math and she knew it wasn't his. So I told her that he was sneaking over and doing me while she was asleep. For twenty-eight years I accused my ex-husband of being a deadbeat dad who refused to acknowledge his son. I even filed a paternity suit against him, but I didn't show up for the blood tests. It worked for all those years until my son called him and asked if he would take a DNA test. I was on the road when I got a call about the results, and I almost wrecked my car. The test proved that I was a liar. That was bad enough, but then his girlfriend sent the DNA results to everyone on my 'friends' list. My friends and family blew up my phone wanting answers. A lie never dies—it will always bite you in the ass!"
    Carrie F. 53
    former groupie

"Lying is merely the skillful and delicate manipulation of a set of circumstances and their predetermined effects on another's perception of them. Put *that* in your book!"
    Cecily Q. 41
    forensic technician

tried and true lies
reliable old standards and threadbare one-liners

"I just want to find a guy who can make me laugh."
    Billie H. 26
    hotel desk clerk

"My new boobs?—I just wanted to do something nice for myself."
    Karin J. 32
    hairstylist

"Well—maybe just *one* little one."
    Tigger N. 82
    retired saloonkeeper

"I can't believe how my body reacts to your touch."
    Annette M. 33
    photographer

THE ROUGHNECK *or* THE POET?

"Oh baby, baby, you're the best I ever had."
    Betsy V. 42
    dog groomer

"I can't remember anything that happened—somebody must have drugged me."
    Bertie K. 24
    student

"It wasn't my fault—I was just along for the ride."
    Amanda S. 34
    exotic dancer

"He raped me."
    Julia C. 18
    student

"All the good ones are already taken."
    Selma R. 37
    ranch foreman

"I just want a man to love me for who I am."
    Jerry Y. 54
    shopping mall security

"I love you so much."
    Kelly A. 55
    high-school teacher

"Don't worry about the money, baby—if we have to we'll just live on love."
    Ashley T. 41
    flight attendant

"I'd live in a tent with you, as long as we can be together."
    Candi J. 39
    firearms dealer

"Don't worry about my weight—it's just nerves. It'll fall right off after the wedding."
    Sabrina N. 37
    dietician

"*Of course* I'm supposed to wear a white wedding dress."
    Alexis Q. 23
    art teacher

"I take you to be my wedded husband, to love and cherish... *blah, blah, blah.*"
    Tyra F. 37
    physical-education teacher

"I've never really done this before."
    Patience A. 39
    assistant district attorney

"Oh, God—oh, God—oh, *God!*"
    Estrella S. 19
    web model

"Oh my god, baby—no one ever made me feel the way you do."
    Adrienne P. 29
    kitchen appliance sales

"Oh, sweetie—*girls night out* is just a bunch of us gabbing about our husbands and kids. It's just good clean fun."
    Connie W. 28
    customer service representative

"Honey, he's just a guy I work with."
    Emmy T. 32
    ski instructor

"It's not like I meant to do it."
    Sophie E. 22
    student

"I just can't love you like you love me."
    Jasmine W. 46
    data analyst

"It's not you, baby—it's me."
    Phoebe F. 31
    pharmacist

"He molested our kids."
    Ellen I. 37
    theme park dancer

13 jealousy

"Jealousy is one thing all women have in common. I've seen it in 2-year-olds. There's a territorial animal in us that hasn't evolved. Jealousy grows with us, and if we're lucky it doesn't get out of control. If it gets away from us we can be killers. It's the cavewoman in us, so be careful."

Drew R. 56
psychology professor

"When my boyfriend finally asked me to marry him I was happier than I'd ever been. I was the last of my circle of friends to get engaged—I was the old spinster. A week before the wedding, a girlfriend invited me to get a manicure to celebrate my engagement. While we were having our nails done she asked if my fiancé had been married before. I told her that he had, and she said I was in for a treat—the sex on our wedding night would be fantastic because he was so experienced. I never felt jealousy until that moment, and it was horrible. I knew right then that our marriage would fail because all I could think of was his ex-wife in bed with him. We stayed married for three years, and then divorced. I was miserable the whole time. I was totally crippled by that vision of them together, and I gained over a hundred pounds."

Ann M. 43
church choir director

"Oh, yeah—I know jealousy. I left my husband to run off with his best friend. I was already remarried when my ex started dating, and I didn't want my kids around her. They decided to get married, and I went crazy! We knew the same people and they told me she was a virgin. If my ex-husband thought he was going to replace me with a virgin, he had fight on his hands. I had seen a TV movie about a mother who accused her ex of molesting the kids, so I did it too. He didn't see our boys for over a year because the courts were so slow. When they finally granted him visitation rights, we moved away. They're grown up now, and they still hate him."
Kelsey M. 28
dishwasher

"My daughter was only three and she was already a *Daddy's girl*. My husband picked her up at daycare and she ran to him screaming 'Daddy!' It was always like she hadn't seen him for weeks. Another little girl without a father ran after her and jumped in my husband's arms. My daughter tensed up and gave him the dirtiest look. The girl put her hands on his cheeks and said 'I wish you were *my* daddy.' When they got home my daughter had a really sour face, so I asked her what was wrong. She cried and said that Daddy didn't love her anymore. She went on and on about the little girl who was going to take her daddy away. The next day she took a pair of kid's safety scissors and cut chunks out of the little girl's hair! She didn't want Daddy to pick her up at daycare again."
Cathy H. 28
graphic designer

"I used to think my jealousy made a man feel more important. After my divorce I did a lot of reading about it, and I guess it's more like torture than it is cute. I punished my husband for something he never did, or ever would have done. I try to control it, but sometimes it feels impossible. The books I read were right—I punished him for my delusions about what another woman was thinking. That's why he left."
Camilla Y. 34
box-office sales

"When I worked for a cell-phone company, every employee got phones with unlimited service for $5 a month. We all got them for ourselves and our husbands. The husbands didn't know that their wives had access to the call records with just a mouse-click. Within a week, three of my co-workers caught their husbands having affairs. They actually called the women and introduced themselves. I got one for my husband, but he he hated cell phones. Then my jealousy really kicked in. For months everyone at work was searching those call records for secret girlfriends. Some of them would check their husband's records ten times a day. A hundred women were in a jealousy-fueled panic because three men had cheated. I was convinced that my husband was having an affair because he wouldn't accept that phone, so I started looking for evidence in his wallet and glovebox. He thought I'd gone crazy. When administration found out what was going on, they stopped the program and changed the rules. Are women more jealous in groups?—*Hell, yeah!*"

Tia S. 43
former office worker

"The best way to fuck with another woman is to build a fire under her jealousy. If you listen carefully she will tell you where her soft spot is, and then you pounce! I broke up a shitload of marriages that way. If they just kept their mouth shut, nobody would know where their goat is tied. But if they're gonna brag about how good their home life is, they're fair game."

Shirley I. 37
office manager

"I had my jealousy under control for a long time, until a beautiful new salesgirl walked through our door. I'm the one who invited her, but she didn't sound so beautiful on the phone. Our business was just getting started and we wanted to run some TV commercials, so the station sent us this siren. She walked in and I felt like I was melting. She was six feet tall and thin, with gorgeous skin and perfect long hair, and wearing some expensive tailored business outfit. I was five-foot-five and eighty pounds overweight, my hair was short and fried from grocery-store haircoloring left on too long, and I wore some leftover lunch on my T-shirt. I was mad at my husband for weeks. Really, he couldn't have given a rat's ass what she looked like. The stupid bastard loves me and he thinks I'm pretty. He was tired of me looking outside our marriage for things to fight over. He was right."

Erika F. 36
business owner

THE ROUGHNECK *or* THE POET?

"My jealousy started when I went to work in an office with other women. I was happy with my husband and our life. I never thought their problems would affect me, but they did. I was becoming suspicious of my husband, and he knew something was wrong. He'd always ask 'What's the matter, baby?' He'd hug me and kiss me and help me with dinner, and at first I'd snap out of it. In a few months I was just mad all the time. One of the women caught her husband having an affair, and she said it was stupid to think our husbands weren't doing the same thing. I got so paranoid I started checking his computer and going through his pockets, and smelling his clothes for signs of another woman. One night he caught me sniffing his underwear, and I went crazy! I badgered him for his girlfriend's name and how long he'd been sleeping with her. I finally quit my job and we got some counseling. Jealousy is worse than drug addiction or alcoholism. Thank God he loved me enough to go through all that."

Fay D. 39
stay-at-home mom

"I was jealous when my ex-husband spoke Spanish. He was the only one at work who was bilingual, and of course most of the Spanish-speaking customers were women. They would call him to translate, and the women were surprised by a white guy speaking Spanish. No matter what age they were, they all acted like giddy teenagers. I couldn't stand to hear them giggle with him. I said some horrible things to him about it, and I made his life hell until he agreed to get a different job. I thought it would fix my jealousy, but it didn't. I just found new things to be jealous about. I go to bed full of hate. I'm afraid one day I'll wake up and find him gone, and I wouldn't blame him."

Suzy L. 29
housewife

"I worked with nine other women, and I was old enough to be their mother. Out of the blue they hired a man about my age. He was forty-seven and gray at the temples, a real gentleman, and the single parent of a very polite 9-year-old daughter. The girls all said he was perfect for me, but I knew he'd rather have a younger woman. He asked me out and we got along really well, but I couldn't understand why he didn't prefer one of the young girls. We fell in love and moved in together, and it was perfect—he even opened a business for me. After a year my jealousy finally got the best of me, and I started to say the stupidest things. I asked him if he'd ever slept with any of the girls in the office. He was shocked and asked me how I could think that. I don't know why, but I bluffed and told him one of the girls had bragged about it. He was furious, and he picked up the phone to call and confront her. I had to admit my lie, and then he was even more shocked. It only got worse, until we finally separated. Jealousy ruined every relationship I ever had."

Nora Q. 48
retail sales

"You ain't seen a jealous woman until you've seen me in action. I get *totally* crazy and nobody can stop me. I used to be engaged to a man who loved me with all his heart—he'd have done anything for me. My jealousy kicked in when this 19-year-old girl started working with me. She was young and fucking perfect. She rode a bicycle everywhere and went to a gym. I hated her because my guy rode one too. He was forty-seven and he could still ride a hundred miles a day. All I could think about was him riding around with her laughing, stopping somewhere and spreading out a blanket, and fucking her 19-year-old brains out! *Shit!*—I'm getting mad just thinking about it. I thought I'd try getting in shape to compete with her, and I started riding my fiancé's bike. After two blocks my legs were so sore I couldn't walk for a week. I called off the wedding and left him, and he never did a damn thing but love me. That's what jealousy does."

Phyllis J. 36
receptionist

"I got so jealous I ended up checking myself into a mental-health facility. My husband was tired of being treated like shit, so he ran me off. We were divorced and I met a new guy who loved me and my two daughters, and I swore I was done with jealousy. My 3-year-old fell in love with him and was always in his arms wherever we went. She would hug his neck so tight, he'd let go of her and she would just hang there. Everyone thought it was cute but me—*I* was supposed to be the center of attention. I was so jealous of my daughter that I gave her to my ex-husband. She's ten now, and I almost never see her. She has a stepmother she calls Mom."

Lizzy F. 37
unemployed

"That's why I show so much cleavage—to make other women jealous. Couples come through the lobby all the time, and I make sure my perky tits and my lacy pushup bra is in their face. They act all arrogant and look down on me because I don't own a mansion on the fairway. They're both bitchy when they come in, but the man leaves happy and the old hag wants to kill him and me both."

Blair T. 27
country club receptionist

"I put my poor husband through six kinds of hell, but he got even with me. I was sick and twisted with jealousy, and I targeted this young girl named Laura. I decided that when he finally did cheat on me, it would be with her. Nothing he could say could get her off my mind. For three years I acted just a little mad, so he knew I hated her existence. Some days were really bad, and I would go to bed mad and turn away from him. He said I was aloof—like I couldn't care less if he died, and I didn't argue. One night I guess he'd had enough. He rolled me over and looked me in the eyes, and said he had to confess—'I slept with Laura.' There aren't any words to tell you how sick I felt. It was nothing like I had imagined—like I'd been kicked in the stomach. I couldn't breathe and I couldn't speak, and I thought I was going to throw up all over him. He looked at me straight-faced for I don't know how long, and then jumped out of bed laughing his ass off. He turned on the light and hollered '*Gotcha!*' I never mentioned her name again."

Samantha T. 38
veterinary assistant

"Holy god! What woman wouldn't be jealous with all these waifish young tramps sleeping with every man they can get their grubby little hands on? My husband is fifty-one, and still really good looking. I can't leave him alone in the grocery store for five minutes before some little slut is all over him! Jealousy is just awareness of the threat."

Joan H. 46
business owner

"My ex-husband was a hairstylist too. I guess I should have known better, but I hated watching him work on women. I put up with it for a few years before I melted down. Jealousy doesn't care if it pays the bills or puts a roof over my head. It's vicious and self-

destructive. I'd be jealous of his customers and what they'd done and accomplished, and I'd eat everything in sight. I put on weight and got jealous of his skinny customers. Then I decided I looked old, and I was jealous of his young customers! I said to him 'I'd rather come home and find you nut-deep in some strange woman, in our bed, than to sit here and watch you laugh with your customers.' I told people I left him because of his job, but really it was my jealousy."
Elsa C. 30
unemployed

"You want to make a woman jealous?—find a wife from some other country. The very thought of some man who's not being tortured by an American woman drives them out of their minds. Even if a mail-order bride is happy, we'll try to free her from her bondage. Women are extremely territorial. We might not want you, but we don't want them to have you either. We'll make you pay—*live with it,* buddy."
Lucille O. 48
real estate broker

"I'm embarrassed. When I met my husband, he was in flight school earning his commercial pilot's license. Well, in a pilot's logbook there's a place for notes after each entry. He was married before, and years ago he'd been flying with his wife and wrote something like 'Barbara, local, landing practice' in the notes. After I saw her name in his old logbook, I refused to fly with him again until he whited-out her name. That was the beginning of my jealousy, and it got much worse. If you want to know whether or not a marriage will last, just look for jealousy—ours didn't survive it."
Hope G. 32
convenience store clerk

"I know why *I'm* jealous. When I was young I thought I could have any guy I wanted because my only competition was other virgins, and not many of them. Then I got drunk at a party. I still had only been with one man—not much competition. As the number grew, I lost my competitive edge and it dawned on me that I had nothing *but* competition anymore. That's how jealousy is born."
Miranda Y. 34
wedding videographer

"I found the cure for jealousy—a new boyfriend. I'm good in the beginning because nobody can compete with new—so I'm *always* new. The best way to get over a man is to get under a new one."
Jill J. 29
emergency medical technician

"Women don't just experience jealousy—they do their best to make other women feel it too."
Doris E. 58
vocational school director

"There are two kinds of jealousy—stupid and not stupid. If you're with a stupid woman, she'll drive you crazy with her jealousy-driven anger. If you're with an intelligent woman, she'll stop at nothing to burn your life to the ground. I mean, there is no kind of evil she won't engage in to ruin you."
Claudia R. 42
retail manager

14 out of my league

"The *'league system'* is more important than you think. Men age better than women so we need a man older than we are, but we don't want people to think he's our father. We need him to look good, but not too good, and not for too long. He's got to fall apart faster than we do or people will think we're his mother. If he's athletic and we're not, he's out. It's okay if we're in shape even if he isn't, because we like the option to get fat and quit going to the gym if we want. Any man better than we are will make us look bad, and he's out of our league—and that's where he should stay. See why women are crazy?"
Virginia O. 46
art history professor

"My mom's always asking me why I don't date a decent man. She doesn't understand that a good-looking guy with a good job is way out of my league. It's easier to hook up with some guy who's not too handsome, and struggling financially—someone who'd be grateful to have me. I'd rather be with a man who thinks I could have done better than *him*, than to have him think he could have done better than *me*."
Ava B. 32
personal secretary

"I'll have sex with a man who has looks and money, but that's all—*just* sex. A few guys have wanted to marry me, but I'm not into torture. All their wives worry about is a younger woman stealing him away. If he's got money and looks, he's arm candy for a night. Let the skinny blondes worry themselves sick."

Summer W. 31
pool maintenance

"I got married really young when my husband made minimum wage. He was a hard worker and he always tried to be a better breadwinner. He kept getting better, higher-paying jobs and the better he did, the more I hated him. He was proud of himself, but I wasn't. I married a kid with no money and he became a professional in five years. I know he did it for me, but I didn't ask him to. So I took the kids away from him and married an alcoholic. That's just the way things work."

Bonita V. 41
waitress

"Wild animals are smart enough to procreate with the most capable males of their species, but women have devolved to the point of consciously seeking out the least worthy men available. They do it because they're lazy and they don't want to do the work needed to earn the favor of a good man. I've heard *'It's easier'* from hundreds of women. These are not just opinions. I hold class five days a week in a forum of nearly four hundred students, most of whom are women. We have open forums each week, and we've addressed this topic over and over. Sadly, it's getting worse—not better."

Shelley K. 54
college professor

"I always have to be with a man I can best intellectually. I need the advantage because I hate losing an argument. I've slept with some real losers, but I've never lost a fight."

Elizabeth R. 53
chiropractic massage therapist

"Get this!—my brother got all clean-cut when he was trying to get a new job. He was hurt because women stopped noticing him. He finally got a job running heavy equipment and it didn't matter how he looked, so he grew back his mustache and—*Nothing!* Somebody said he looked like a cop, so he grew out his hair and his beard and the ladies wouldn't leave him alone! He couldn't believe it. He wore a dirty old cowboy hat and he looked like he hadn't bathed in a week, and women at the bar bought him all the beer he could drink. I had to explain to him why they like the bad-boy look. That's the 'league system'—right?"

Cheryl U. 31
mobile-home park manager

"You don't understand what it's like to be with a really good-looking guy who has a nice car. Everywhere we went the women were like vultures. They'd come right up to him and start flirting, even if I was holding his arm. It's like he was some kind of drug! I felt invisible. He never went out on me, but I hated all the attention he got. I'd rather be with a guy no one else wants."

Karlee E. 20
retail clerk

"Listen, I know exactly what you mean. It got so bad for me that when I started gaining this weight, I actually dated a man who was homeless. I asked him out and he was flabbergasted! I bought him clean clothes so I could take him out in public. He didn't want to work or better himself, so I finally ended it. I remember when I looked pretty hot and I had much higher standards. Now my mirror decides the kind of men I date. I choose a man nobody will stare at and wonder what he's doing with the fat pig."

Kathy S. 54
funeral director

"I've been there too. I really liked this guy in my Psych class and we flirted the whole semester. We were both smart and we had the highest scores in the class. Our final was an essay, and when our professor handed out the scores he laid them face-down on our desks. When he got to my friend he shook his head as he put the paper down. I felt sorry for him. I had scored 48 out of 50 points, which was an 'A'. I followed my friend outside and I just had to ask. He handed me his essay, and the professor had written *'perfect score—Congrats!'* He'd gotten a 50. I never spoke to him again—is that what you're talking about?"

Alison Y. 28
college dropout

"Why am I with him?—well, I guess it's because I have nothing to lose. If he dumps me I won't have a broken heart."
Danielle T. 28
bookkeeper

"Sure, there are men *and* women who aren't worth a shit—who doesn't know that? Isn't that why we're supposed to choose wisely?"
Nicole A. 43
auto parts sales

"Dumb guys and fat guys make the best prey. They want to please a woman so much they'll do anything for you, and you can sleep with them if they don't gross you out—or not, if they do. They'll always take you out again, sex or not."
Sissy N. 44
fuel attendant

"Losers have nothing to complain about—they get laid way more often than the decent men. So keep buying us those drinks, guys!"
Cassandra W. 24
tattoo artist

"My parents and all my friends tried to stop me from marrying this idiot, but I wouldn't listen. He was a drunken asshole in high school, but he didn't go for the cheerleaders so I thought I wouldn't have much competition—I was right about that. When we go to parties he gets shitfaced and digs in his nose for a booger, puts it on his shoulder and walks around introducing everyone to his 'little friend.' Can you believe I had children with him?"
Peyton Q. 35
optometry assistant

"Women should take a lesson from my horses. I've paid tens of thousands of dollars for stud service to make sure my mare's bloodline gets better—not worse. What's *wrong* with women?! If I bred my horses the way women breed, I'd be broke and I'd have to put the animals down."
Shirley S. 49
horse breeder

"Women bitch about not having any good men left to choose from, and it's all lies. We all have stories about at least one fantastic guy who had a burning desire for us. But we run like hell because we don't want him to know that we probably fucked half the men he works with. It happened to me, and *damn* it was awkward. We slink around with the worst guys we can find and leave the true romantics out in the cold, because it's safer."

Renee T. 23
hospitality hostess

"I was tired of working and I had to choose from fat, ugly, stupid, old, or crippled—just not poor. I didn't want to work so poor was not an option. I chose old with money. In a few years I got what I wanted and divorced him. I got child-support, alimony, and a permanent babysitter."

Denise F. 34
unemployed

"I didn't choose him for love—I married him for the money. I can find love anywhere, but the bank account is what matters most. Women aren't stupid."

Lisa B. 49
bookkeeper

"I get hit on all the time, but how I react depends on how I feel at the time. I mostly feel fat and ugly so I usually sleep with losers who promise not to call me after."

Kelly H. 34
taxi driver

"Women used to fight over the best possible husband. They would dress their best, learn to cook, and above all be a virgin on their wedding night. Those three things used to be all a woman needed to make a good man feel obligated for life. Now most women don't have a prayer of attracting a good man."

Martha K. 73
widow (married 53 years)

"I thought that because my husband isn't the best-looking man I could avoid the attacks from my co-workers, but it didn't work. Every chance they get, they start prowling. It's not so much how a husband looks as it is how happy they think I am—that's what they go after. My husband is a really nice man, but I married him for all the wrong reasons. I settled on him just to be safe, and I'm not."

Molly R. 25
swap-meet manager

"These women settle for the biggest loser they can find, and then have kids with him. What are they thinking? Do they really believe his genetics won't influence how their kids turn out? Not only will they have all his undesirable traits, but his family will be a major influence for the rest of their lives. Is his family going to encourage them to go to college and live a decent life? They need to think about that before they drop their panties."
Maryellen C. 62
decorative & faux-finish painter

"It's because most of us are fat, and fat girls will sleep with anyone. If many more women get fat, there won't be enough men to go around. That will be a catfight to remember."
Tara S. 37
hospice volunteer

"I fell for this one guy when we first met. I thought he was gorgeous. He was rough-looking with a beard and long hair—like the Marlboro man, only better. He was a mechanic and usually covered with grease, which worked for me. He asked me out for a date at a really nice restaurant, but when he came to pick me up he had trimmed his beard and mustache really short and gotten a haircut—I hated it! He was still handsome, but not my type anymore. He asked me out again but I wouldn't go."
Sheila N. 30
county worker

"Women date losers, and then they congregate at work to complain about them. Why would they purposely choose a man they can't stand to be with?—why not find somebody they won't always be mad at? I don't get it, but it happens all the time."
Olivia H. 34
county dispatcher

"It's a no-brainer for me. I need a tall, fat man to make me look smaller—that's my system. The bigger I get, the bigger he needs to be. I have to have sex with them or they wander off. I've gone through three of them so far, and if I get any bigger I may have trouble finding one big enough."
Christy W. 46
plus-size clothing sales

"My daughter's husband is like that—talk about a mismatched pair. Bless his heart, but he can't find his ass with both hands and a map! The poor kid can't form a sentence to save his life, and he has no desire to educate himself. She was an honor student and she defends her choice to the end. This is where my grandkids are going to come from?—help me Jesus!"

Traci P. 47
high-school teacher

"I sit in the mall and watch the people-watchers. They always comment on the beautiful women with the goofiest looking men, and I overhear them say 'He *must be hung*' or 'Trust *fund!*' Even total strangers can see what's happening to women."

Cindy A. 56
retail sales associate

"My mother started dating a man who's in prison for murder—it's mind boggling! I'm afraid her brain has gone out to lunch for the last time. She acts like a schoolgirl when she talks about him, and she got a part-time job after work to send him money. Help me with this—*What the fuck?!* If I try to talk to her about it, she walks away. I didn't know she was hard-up enough to date a man she'll never even see. I guess there are lots of women doing it, though."

Elise A. 31
florist

"I want a man who's always in trouble. If he's always doing the right thing, he's gonna expect the same from me, and that ain't gonna happen. I need to remind him of the last six things he did wrong so he can't find fault with me. That's why we look for the bad boys."

Lupe K. 30
social worker

"It's perfectly natural to lower your standards when your looks start fading. After forty-five, most women can't go to the singles' bar and walk out with a man their own age. It's either a 60-year-old or some kid who heard that older women know some tricks. I'm not surprised by any of it."

Marjorie L. 51
advertising account executive

"My sister whines about how she worked for ten years putting her husband through medical school, and how he ran off with a nurse. It's total *bullshit!* My sister loved being married to a starving student who depended on her. When he started making money, which was the plan—*Helloooo!*—she freaked out and started treating him like shit. He tried to reason with her, but she couldn't handle his success and she ran him off. I watched it happen, and she still denies it. Everywhere she goes she tells the same story and gets women all pissed-off at men. I don't see her anymore, but my former brother-in-law is still my doctor."

Maggie V. 48
registered nurse

the list compiled by Emma from multiple contributors

"We made this list for you, ranking the kinds of partners women will choose, depending on how lazy, desperate or damaged they think they are—starting with the most desirable."

1. unfaithful—*handsome*
2. stupid—*not ugly*
3. stupid—*ugly*
4. old guy—*credit card*
5. old guy—*no credit card*
6. alcoholic—*employed*
7. alcoholic—*unemployed*
8. drug addict
9. drug dealer
10. wife beater
11. sex offender
12. parolee—*nonviolent*
13. parolee—*violent*
14. inmate—*less than 10 years remaining*
15. inmate—*10 years to life*
16. death-row inmate
17. your best girlfriend's ex-husband
18. your best girlfriend

Emma R. 31
bartender

15 relationships & marriage

"To be in a successful relationship I think you need to actually enjoy being in one, and most of us don't. How could anyone stand being with the same man their whole life?"
Kate R. 25
cocktail waitress

"Being married doesn't make me happy. If I'm ever happy it's in spite of my marriage. A good wife never lets her misery show. That's what's wrong with most married women—they want to make their husbands as miserable as they are. If you just leave a man alone, he won't bother you as much. I have it down to a science."
Nina R. 51
caterer

"Marriage is fattening. I had the cutest figure when I got married, and now I'm as big as a house! I know I eat too much, but it's not just the food. There's something about getting a man to commit that makes me lazy. My husband wants us to have a baby, but I'm afraid if I get pregnant I won't stop growing. A baby would be more work and I can't find the energy to clean the house as it is. I've turned into a slob!"
Karyn C. 29
housewife

"When women have a man interested in an actual relationship, the first thing they do is consult with other women at least as screwed-up as they are."
Lauren N. 37
office worker

"I'm married to a good man and I love him, but I'm not *in* love with him—you know what I mean? I'll probably leave him when the kids are a little older so I can get on with my life."
Sandra Y. 28
insurance company receptionist

"I warned my daughter to never expect happiness from a marriage —that's not what marriage is for. She didn't listen, and she's been disappointed with all three of her husbands."
Patty V. 59
store manager

"Never marry a man you've been friends with—he knows all your dirt and you'll never get away with lying to him. I married a really good friend and I'd forgotten all the stuff I told him years before. Without thinking, I started my bullshit about not having been overly promiscuous, and trying to act like a good girl. He looked at me like I was crazy, but he let me talk. When I finished my sales pitch he reminded me word-for-word of the stories I'd told him about my party years and my wild sexual past. I honestly forgot I had told him all that stuff. I was embarrassed, and he was hurt that I tried to lie to him. I guess it was just habit."
Liza G. 42
cook

"I can't believe how much things have changed in my short lifetime. During the Vietnam war a lot of young girls were left with children and a flag. It was an honorable thing for a man to consider choosing a young widow and her children to be his family. Women of all ages would offer congratulations, and call the man lucky for finding a 'ready-made family.' Now the best advice in that situation is to run like the wind! Stepfathers have been vilified by the media and the collective mind of women. If a stepfather doesn't allow his adopted family to do exactly as they please, he'll be falsely accused of everything from mental cruelty to sexual abuse. There's no hope for a stable, disciplined upbringing. I grew up with a stepfather and when he passed, I grieved. He loved me like his own and I regarded him as my father. I revered his position, and I don't know whether it was learned or it was taught to me. Either way, I wish I could bottle it and share it with our whole country."

June S. 59
school superintendent

"I married a 70-year-old man who takes care of my two children from a previous marriage. I service him on the weekdays and I get to do what I want on the weekends. I have boyfriends my own age, and it works for both of us."

Carol Z. 34
hairstylist

"Men have a hard time because women all act like angels, but most aren't. It's easier for a woman to know what she's getting into because men are just themselves more easily than women are."

Toni E. 19
student

"My daughter spent a year planning for her wedding—not that a wedding requires a year to orchestrate, it just takes that long to bum enough money from people to pay for it. When my son-in-law kissed the bride and the applause died down, the crowd headed for the bar and the food. My daughter stood there as everyone walked away, and she said 'That's it?—all the money we spent, and that's it?' I tried to tell her that the money was also for the marriage, and hopefully that will last longer than the wedding."

Marie D. 45
uniform sales

"I want a man with enough balls to control me and give me a good reason to submit. It's not my fault if he's weak—I blame men for how I am. If I can get away with it, I'll do it. When a man tries to treat me like a lady, he's just a wimp and a big turn-off."

Gwen J. 29
deli manager

"I'll sleep with a guy on the first date, but it depends on what kind of girl I want him to think I am. If I really like him and I want a relationship, I'll make him wait."

Amy T. 18
unemployed

"Here is the best lesson on relationships anyone can ever give or receive: Women start, maintain, and end all relationships—period! The first thing a woman wants to do is argue this fact, but after thinking about it they say 'Hmmm,' and finally agree, if they're not brain-dead."
Alice A. 48
grocery clerk

"Ever since high school I've gone back and forth from really thin to really fat. I swear, when I'm skinny I'm so horny I could do a football team. So I find a boyfriend and everything is great until I start putting the weight back on. My boyfriends have never been mean to me when I get fat. As a matter of fact, most of them liked it. The problem is me—I think I'm gross when I'm fat, and I'm not horny anymore so I break up with them. My last boyfriend bought a motorcycle and he came over to take me for a ride. He almost needed a crane to get me on it. When I finally got on, my ass took up the whole seat and he was sitting on the gas tank. I told him to lose my phone number. I'm starting a new diet tomorrow."
Leticia G. 46
taxi dispatcher

"Most of us aren't even qualified to be in a relationship! In a real relationship two people need to depend on each other. How can someone depend on their spouse and be independent at the same time? We just use word-salad to talk our way out of our responsibility to another person. It works until someone wants to break their commitment. I've been to five weddings in three years, and four of the couples are now either fighting or separated. Marriage is not a joke—the people getting *married* are the joke. If I get married I'm going to make sure I know what the hell I'm doing."
Monique A. 27
electronics

"I went to nursing school expressly to marry a doctor so I didn't ever have to work again. I fantasized about it all the way through college. When I started working in the hospital I found out that everyone else wanted to marry a doctor too! I guess I didn't get that memo."
Florence L. 30
registered nurse

"When I'm in a relationship I don't care if he has sex with another woman—I just better not find out about it. If it gets back to me, he wasn't being discreet. That's my rule. I'd rather he took care of his needs somewhere else than to have him chasing me around all the time."

Brandy V. 40
tailor

"I've been married for three years and I've never been so, like, disappointed in my whole life. I thought it would be magical all the time. It's hard work living with another person. I wish I could move back in with my parents and get my freedom back. I should've, like, waited."

Emily O. 23
bookstore sales associate

"If men suffer from the Peter Pan syndrome, what do you call a grown woman who can't stop asking her father for money? All our daughter has to do is whine, and *Daddy* reaches for his wallet. She doesn't want us to tell her husband that we give her money, and that makes me so uncomfortable. I know that keeping secrets and living beyond her means will eventually destroy her marriage."

Valerie B. 54
cafeteria worker

"The best relationship I ever had was with a married man. It's a lot less work than having your own husband. I doubt that I'll ever get married because there will always be somebody like me trying to move in on him."

Adele E. 31
home healthcare

"A relationship is something that's built by a man and a woman. It's not something to stand back and look at, wondering if it's still attractive or not. It's work!"

Blake A. 45
family business

"Just give me an ugly guy with a good job. That's the only kind of relationship that will last. When I'm ready to settle down, that's exactly what I'm going to look for."

Carina H. 33
elementary schoolteacher

"A woman's heart is supposed to be a storehouse of love and concern for her man and her children. Now look at them—they're just boiling with hatred and competitiveness, and it's all directed toward men. It's such a waste."
Rita C. 51
sales

"What happened to courting a woman? How the hell is a relationship ever going to work if there's no courting? These girls are in bed with a man on the first date! When I was young we understood that you can't get to know the important things about a man when you're in bed with him. Young men used to have to cross the tracks to find these kinds of girls, and they weren't looking for a wife when they did."
Angela Y. 76
retired

"You can't find a man worth marrying if you think you already know everything about men. That's just being lazy. There are as many different kinds of men as there are men on the planet. Women get together and swap a few stories from TV shows and they think they're experts. Why not just put on a blindfold and run across the street?"
Victoria M. 69
retired geologist

"Women have always been able to fool a man with a pretty face and a line of bullshit. A woman's power over a man is like a gun—it can be used for good or evil. If a woman ends up in a stupid situation, she only has herself to blame. Women should have listened to their mothers and grandmothers. We could have shown them how to use their power to make something good."
Pamela T. 64
secretary

"Have you ever listened to a group of girls in their twenties giving each other advice about relationships? It's the most terrifying experience I've ever had! These imbeciles can own guns and drive cars, and they're out there running loose. The scariest thing about it is that someday one of these Einsteins might be the mother of my grandchildren. I heard them in the break room at work, and the big debate was whether to have sex with a man on the first or the second date! They were so serious—you'd think they were discussing quantum physics! Is this really our future?"

Alana G. 52
office manager

"I tell a man right up front how many guys I've fucked, and that there's a good chance I already fucked his best friend. I make him a promise that while we're together I'll be with him, and only him. He has to promise not to ask me to marry him, but I can keep him around a lot longer than most women could. Men *like* being told the truth—it puts them at ease."

Liz Q. 35
barista

"When I'm out with my husband we always hold hands, and women can't seem to help asking us how long we've been together. We must attract attention because we look older than dirt. I tell them in my shaky voice that we just celebrated our fifty-sixth wedding anniversary, and they say 'Awwww.' They never fail to ask the second question, 'What's the secret?' I straighten right up, look them in the eye and say *'Don't be a whore!'*"

Claire D. 77
retired philosopher

"No marriage will last unless a man and a woman commit to making it on their own without their parents' help—ever! I don't care if it means living in their car or living on food stamps. Suffering the bad times together makes a marriage stronger and it teaches people to survive—not just in the world, but in the marriage, too. Every dollar a married couple gets from their parents is poison. Somewhere down the road they should be able to embrace each other and say 'We made it!' Without that accomplishment a marriage will just be another chore."

Lucy K. 57
loan officer

"Women read about romance and watch movies about it, but they refuse to subscribe to it. If they did believe in romance they'd be ostracized by their friends, and especially their mothers. Most of them can't afford to be more than romantic voyeurs."

Desiree I. 48
web designer

"I always thought this thing [pointing to her vagina] would at least get me a car and a house. I really believed that when I was done using it to get free drinks and dinner, I'd just wash it off real good and put it on the market to snag a man with a good job. I was shocked when I found out mine wasn't the youngest or the prettiest one around anymore."
Lacy T. 37
veterinary technician

"It's hard to find a relationship if you're fat. I used to go on a diet when I was looking for a man—now I just go to the tanning booth. Men like skinny, but they also like a woman with a tan. They have a sign at the tanning salon that says 'If you can't lose it, tan it.' That's my new motto."
Tami M. 49
dressmaker

"When all of us from work go out, we have to sit and listen to the fat girls complain about not being able to find a relationship. They've read too many of those *big & beautiful* magazines. We try to be nice and ignore that their asses are so big they're sitting on two chairs, but sisters—please! We recommend trying a new perfume or a new haircut just to shut them up. We're so mean! Bottom line—fat affects your love life. I don't care how pretty their face is, a man doesn't wanna flop around on a woman that's built like a waterbed."
Katya A. 36
office manager

"A man who loves his wife will chase her around for sex long after her body has gone bad. But when *his* body starts showing age we find him repulsive. It's to the point where I'd rather he had sex with the widow next door, as long as they don't make a scene about it. That's the difference between men and women."
Annabelle B. 67
retired nurse

"Women used to be the ones who made a relationship work, and they loved doing it. Now they just sit around *waiting* for it to work, and bitch when it doesn't."
Josie F. 47
public relations

"When we opened our business and started making loads of money, I started eating. I still don't know why. I would tell my husband I was going to the bank to make a deposit, and I'd hit four different fast-food places and toss the wrappers in a dumpster behind the grocery store. I'd walk back in with a diet drink in my hand. I did the math and I was spending $800 a month on junk-food behind my husband's back. When he found out he called it embezzlement, and we got divorced."

Gertie O. 30
unemployed

"I can't be with someone who really loves me. What if I get fat, or my face gets burned off in a car accident? He'll dump me."

Parker J. 35
art-supply store manager

"It's like clockwork—women hit the ground running after about fifteen years. They don't need a babysitter for the kids anymore, so they study the party scene and start trying to make up for lost time. They lose weight, buy new clothes, and get laid by a stranger. It's very predictable."

Lin M. 55
business chamber director

"If you have kids, and he has a good job, your income is guaranteed. *Hellooo*—child support? It's a financial investment."

Damiana E. 38
ex-wife/mother

"I overheard my 17-year-old son asking his father how to get the good-looking girls to pay attention to him. My husband said 'Car and a job, son—car and a job.' I cried."

Dallas R. 39
newspaper editor

16 feminism

"The historical waves of feminism are complicated and their meanings are lost to most women today. They've adopted some of the nomenclature, but they're incorrectly attributing their horrible behaviors to the feminist and women's liberation movements. I doubt that the early activists who sweat blood to ensure equality would approve of the results. The laywomen today who claim to be feminists and liberated women are nothing but a cult, fighting against men with nothing but ignorance."

Pearl W. 50
high-school history teacher

"All that's left of women's liberation is a cold war against men, and we gather in small groups to recruit more terrorists for a cause we don't understand. We sabotage our own futures and any hope of having a strong family of our own. Just ask any feminist where her beliefs come from, and she won't even know. I used to call myself a feminist because I didn't like being called a 'man-hater,' but it's the same thing. A liberated feminist is just an angry, uneducated woman in the workplace who works too much for too little pay, and she doesn't even know why she's mad."

Jane U. 57
courier service owner

"You can't blame the feminist movement for how most women behave. Blame the last three generations of lazy women who decided they were experts because they read a few headlines. Wild sex, partying, and man-hating were never promoted by respectable feminist groups. A little knowledge is dangerous, and that's all most women have when it comes to feminism. If the woman sitting in the bar who left her kids home alone is a feminist, I'm a brain surgeon."

Irene Y. 38
radio newscaster

"Somebody needs to tell these women that the war with men is over, and women lost. They just won't admit it. If women would just realize their value they could reverse this nightmare. It's those bitter, uneducated mothers and grandmothers who were whores in the '60s and '70s who taught their daughters to hate men, and for what? Ask them how many orgies they had—they'll lie. The fight was supposed to win more respect from men, but women decided that sex was more fun. Wild promiscuity cost women any hope for respect from men. Women used to rule the world—now they're workforce minions bowing to the man behind the curtain. Knowledge is power, and today women have neither."

Lorraine D. 59
artist/poet

"My mom is an old women's libber from the '70s and she's the most hateful person I know. She hates my stepdad, and he's a really nice guy. I can't have a man in my life without her telling me how worthless they are. I don't know what she expected from liberation, but it must not have been happiness."

Jayne F. 43
employment office worker

"Feminism is like religion. They say if you don't follow their rules, you will suffer—and they'll make sure you do."

Kirsten H. 37
landscaping

"Women's lib is bullshit! It was just an excuse to be a slut and blame it on men. How was that liberating?"

Myrna W. 63
business owner

"I want a man to love me, and so do all the women I know. I hate women because if I find a man to love me, women hate me for it. So I hate men in public and love them in private. I support women publicly, but hate them privately—that's feminism."
Anna May K. 33
petroleum engineer

"Feminism was supposed to eliminate inequality and promote social change—what a crock of shit! Instead, it turned a nation of housewives into a mob of man-haters with jobs. Their jobs turned them into frantic spenders too busy to get involved in any social cause. A woman with a job is too distracted by a sale on shoes to give a shit about reform, or even about her own children. I dropped out a long time ago."
Jean P. 55
housewife/grandmother

"Women's lib was meant to challenge the notion that women should have different roles from men. Up until then, men and women shared this notion. There were men in high places who had power to make changes, but there were also powerful women who opposed feminism. It took more effort to change the women's minds than it did men's. Feminists of the third wave convinced women that men were having all the sex and all the fun they wanted, and the sisters were deprived. By convincing women to spread their legs, feminists got their foot in the door of women's simple thinking, and man-hating became the rage. It was a perfectly orchestrated propaganda campaign that insidiously sacrificed women's virtue, calling it collateral damage. And we fell for it."
Beverly A. 68
retired schoolteacher

"I thought feminism was supposed to be about equal pay and maternity leave without losing your job. All I've seen is an office full of worn-out old hags who act worse than the men they hate. Most of them spend the weekend drinking, and the rest of the week recovering from a hangover. For a group that claims to hate men, they sure talk about them a lot. When they get laid they brag about it like teenagers—and some of them are married! It's pitiful."
Lindy E. 27
customer support agent

"If being a feminist means I can't love and trust my husband, I don't want to be one. If women spent as much time loving their families as they do complaining, feminism would just fade away."
Priscilla S. 36
homemaker ("and proud of it")

"When I hear women say 'Men do it—so can we,' I ask them 'What men?'—not my man! They think I'm stupid if I don't suspect my husband of sleeping with other women behind my back. They'll date a married man and get pissed-off when they catch the bastard with another mistress. Or they leave the bar with some drunk who doesn't remember them the next day, and then they think they're experts on men. They call themselves 'liberated women.' My grandma always asks me 'If everybody jumped off a cliff, would you?' They need to talk to my grandma."
Brittany J. 25
office worker

"The feminists worked us into a frenzy and caused us to give up our natural ability to be the best thing a man could hope for. I remember being so mad at men, and I didn't have one legitimate reason. What's wrong with being submissive to a man if he's worthy? I don't know a single woman who doesn't have a man for a boss. What's the difference?—they're still submitting to a man. We were young and horribly misled. Our thinking wasn't our own, and in most cases it still isn't."
Bess L. 64
private caregiver

"Women's libbers and feminists make *great* mothers—it only took two generations for them to breed the morality right out of an entire nation of young women. Now our daughters are hard-core, immoral breeding and fucking machines! I know way too many people my age raising grandchildren because their daughters are too busy getting knocked-up again. We should be *so* proud."
Jacqueline N. 56
probation officer

"We tried to punish men into submission so we could be their equals. Well, we still aren't equal and men have adapted just fine to our rebellion. Now men can have sex anytime they want, with just about any woman they want, because we threw away our self-worth for feminism. We showed them, didn't we? In the '60s we burned our bras, which was a man's invention, so they made them in different colors and sewed lace on them and made more millions. Have you noticed we're all wearing bras again? That part of my life was such a waste of time. I only hope my grandchildren don't suffer from the damage we did. I know my daughter has, and it breaks my heart."

Meg T. 66
retired

"Women's lib was supposed to be women joining forces for the good of other women, right? Here's the problem with that—women have always hated each other, even before they turned against men. Any woman who's ever worked with other women would rather teach kindergarten than do it again, because 5-year-olds are more mature. Whoever decided to start a movement that required women to join forces had their head up their ass!"

Kat R. 54
shuttle service driver

"Women think they're fighting against *men* for women's rights—*Bullshit!* To achieve more rights for women a feminist needs to be politically active. Hating and mistreating men is just an excuse to do nothing about a cause they know nothing about. Most women with full-time jobs are useless after an eight-hour day, and they'd rather have a foot massage from a man they don't even like than to get involved—they're lazy."

Joyce C. 52
active member Feminist Majority Foundation

"Feminists crack me the fuck up! I love fucking with them. You can't find a more dedicated group that doesn't know shit about what they believe or why they believe it. They hate men, but they're always looking for one and they know that other women are their worst enemy. Try having a feminist explain her cause and watch her forget how to talk. They're just a bunch of hateful bitches throwing a tantrum because the man they wanted didn't want to marry a whore."

Rebecca V. 39
doctor's wife

"Being a feminist is like getting a tattoo on your belly—when you get old it's inappropriate, and it looks like shit."
Gladys D. 71
retired

"Those old worn-out libbers are still trying to make women hate men. They just don't give up. My niece is always fighting with my sister about men. She's stuck in the '60s, and doesn't want my niece to trust or rely on a man. She badgers her to get a career so when 'the bastard' leaves she won't go hungry. Someday my niece's husband is going to choke his mother-in-law to death, and I wouldn't blame him."
Dorothy J. 54
wife

"We screwed ourselves when we bought into all the women's movements. It was hard enough to attract a good man before—now it's near impossible. And what does a man want with a woman who's always ready to fight?"
Paulette S. 71
retired high-school teacher

"I want a man, but I don't want to need one. My mother beat it into my head to never need a man because they'll always leave you. She calls herself a feminist, but there's nothing feminine about her. I love her to death, but she let herself go twenty years ago. She looks like an old truck driver in her sweats and a flattop haircut. She gets mad at me for wearing makeup, and she says I'm just trying to attract men. Actually, I think she's mad all the time."
Jami Y. 24
motel desk clerk

"Feminism is a great big pile of shit that women stepped in, and they're too stubborn to admit it. *Yeah,* I always wanted to belong to a group that requires its members to be total psycho-bitches and not have a clue what their charter means! If you think those animal-rights activists are brainwashed, try going to a few feminazi meetings. Don't drink the kool-aid, though. Talk about being *out there*—they scared me to death."
Krista O. 39
home-schooling coordinator

"Women's lib was a plane crash, and women are still stumbling around like walking wounded, waiting for the ambulances to arrive. If there was ever a meaning or a point to it, we missed it."
Sylvia T. 57
dry cleaning

"The fight for women's rights was just media hype. They convinced us that men were stupid, so we had to be stupider. Hell, a hundred years ago men didn't want us to smoke, so we rebelled and started smoking. We thought we'd won some kind of battle and we ended up killing ourselves."
Vera E. 68
retired military

"Women have become the laziest people on the planet. They're followers—too lazy to think for themselves and act on their own behalf, or in their own interest. Women were far more powerful before the feminists got in their heads."
Melody B. 64
self-employed

"If feminism was so great, why were so many women taking valium in the '60s and '70s? It turned into an epidemic of pill-popping women because it ran against their natural grain to do what the feminists told them they should do."
Lily A. 67
retired government employee

"All that's left of women's lib is a bunch of feral women who wouldn't listen to their mothers."
Claire J. 58
waitress

"I did everything my feminist mother told me to do. I have a job, a mortgage, a car payment, sexual freedom, and you know what it's worth?—*Not a fucking thing!* She's still not happy, and neither am I."
Kathleen M. 43
college administrator

17 children & parenting

"I have two daughters and I love them both. I really enjoy spending time with my oldest, but I can't stand being around my younger one. We brought them up the same, but my youngest has grown hateful and bitter. No one can understand it—their father is a very sweet man, and I'm reasonably easy to get along with. I used to feel bad about how differently I felt about them, but I got over it."
Catherine K. 54
real estate agent

"I've been a deputy in Los Angeles for twenty-four years. For the last eleven I've worked with juveniles, and you wouldn't believe how many of their mothers used drugs all through their pregnancy. People don't understand that these babies are born abnormal, and missing some basic human emotional capacity. There's a real conviction now that these drug babies are genetically damaged. I work with them every day, and they don't grasp the concepts of right and wrong. They're extremely detached, even sociopathic. It scares the hell out of me because in fifteen or twenty years they'll be adults who can kill without batting an eye."
Meredith F. 53
law enforcement

"Too much is made of adult children living with their parents. It's one thing if your kids are lazy bums and you're feeding them, doing their laundry and cleaning up after them, but if they are helping support the household, financially or otherwise, that's quite another. It's the bad news that always attracts attention, but I'll defend my son's decision to raise his family under our roof. He works hard at his job, but he can't make enough money to buy his own home. He's always helping his dad around the house, and his financial contribution more than pays his family's way. We'll leave the house to our son anyway, and there's plenty of room—why should they wait until after we're gone? If I had my way the extended family would be popular again."

Mary H. 61
homemaker

"We elected the lawmakers who prevent us from disciplining our children, and who convinced us we're abusing the little angels if we don't allow them to make their own decisions. Children and teenagers are starved for guidance and discipline, and they keep testing for it with bad behavior, expecting to find limits. Without boundaries and consequences they end up destroying their lives. We tied our own hands and our young people are paying for it."

Marian T. 70
retired

"I don't know what the hell is happening here. I know a lot of women who left their husbands and gave away their kids, only to go live with alcoholics and drug addicts. They gave them to their parents or ex-husbands and ran away, and the kids feel so abandoned. I've talked with some of them, and they are in shock about what their mothers did."

Vanessa B. 36
teacher's assistant

"I raised my granddaughter for the first five years of her life because my daughter was using drugs and lost custody. I worked hard to get her back on track and off the drugs, and finally the courts granted her custody again. I felt like I was giving away my own child when I delivered my granddaughter back to her mother. I grieved for over a year, and got a second job to keep from going crazy. I sent extra money to help with raising my granddaughter. I started dating a nice man, and my daughter went berserk. She demanded that I break it off with him or she wouldn't let me see or talk to my granddaughter. She was afraid my new relationship would cause me to stop sending money. I was trying to be a loving mother and grandmother, but I created a monster. I gave in to my daughter and broke up with my boyfriend. I quit both my jobs and moved 800 miles to be closer to my girls. Then my daughter was furious that I was no longer working enough to earn extra money to give her. We fought for a couple of weeks and she refused to let me see my granddaughter anyway. My greedy daughter cost me my granddaughter, my boyfriend, both my jobs, and the home I'd always known."

Andrea G. 49
teacher/teen counselor

"I was sure my kids would turn out fine if I didn't work, got them involved in sports, supported all their activities, made time for heart-to-hearts with each of them—and it was a total failure! When they decided to hit the streets with the popular crowd, I was tossed away like garbage. I became a mistreated housemaid for two spiteful hellions. I was lied to, stolen from, and hit in the face for refusing to loan my car to my 16-year-old son who was drinking every day. We consulted a child psychologist, only to be told I was too rigid with my discipline! This sounds bad, but if I had it to do again I would never have had children. Parents don't have the right or the power to make decisions about their own children anymore. My husband will retire in four years, and we're going to leave the country and not tell anyone where we are."

Ruth A. 48
former mother

"Women are the reason kids are so out-of-control. The first step toward screwing up your kid is to treat your husband with disgust and cripple his influence. The kids are over-feminized by their mother, and they don't have the stability that comes from a loving marriage. I wish I had a penny for every time my mom said 'Don't tell your father.' She taught me to disrespect men. If I could have valued my dad's strength and kindness, it would have helped me to choose a better husband. It's a cycle that never stops."

Bev K. 42
hostess

"I was a horrible mother, and I admit it. After I divorced my husband I'd bring a new guy home every week without even thinking about what it would do to my daughter. I guess I thought she'd just raise herself—it didn't occur to me that she'd use me for an example. She was married at eighteen and divorced at nineteen, and she's had more boyfriends than she can count. And get this—I married her dad because he was buying a house. I thought if I stuck around long enough I'd have some equity and he would have to buy me out when I left. I was horrible to everybody because I was mad all the time, and I still don't know why."
Bridget V. 44
unemployed

"We were taught that women didn't need a husband to raise children. The news was full of stories about sperm banks, and even magazines and the movies made it seem like a good choice for independent women. I couldn't afford that so I picked a guy I thought would give me a pretty child, and I dated him for a couple of months until I missed two periods. I broke up with him and he never knew I was carrying his baby. I raised my daughter by myself and all my friends approved, but I think now it was wrong and selfish. I wasn't a good mother and my daughter is as screwed-up as I ever was. She needed a father and I needed a husband, but I was too stubborn to admit it."
Shelly C. 56
self-employed

"If a woman marries the dumbest shit she can find because she's fat or just wants to piss off her parents, she's not going to like her kids very much because they're just copies of the dumbshit. The kids will suffer from minimal parenting, if not outright neglect. There was a time when a mother was feared and dangerous if she thought her kids were threatened, or even insulted, but those days are gone."
Janet W. 58
car dealer

"I taught grade school for twenty-nine years and I've seen what divorce does to our children. It's without a doubt the most devastating form of child abuse. I hope I say this properly, but I believe it's worse than physical and sexual abuse. Don't get me wrong—that kind of abuse *is* horrible, but it's more easily treated than are the long-term effects of losing a parent to divorce. Students who've faced even the *death* of a parent don't seem to suffer as much as those with a parent living on the other side of town. The deep sense of personal rejection is incomprehensible to them. Children are resilient and able to recover from serious trauma with wisdom and understanding beyond their years, but the effects of divorce are chronic and follow them into adulthood. The parents get all the attention while the children suffer silently. The best parents are openly affectionate—they care for their children and love each other completely."

Lois E. 71
retired elementary schoolteacher

"A desperate father brought his daughter to my office and pleaded with me to talk some sense into her. She was thirteen and she thought she was being abused because he wouldn't let her wear revealing clothes to school. I asked her to describe what she wanted to wear, and it would have made a prostitute blush. She had been an honor student, but failing at school had become part of her rebellion against her father. She was about the meanest, most vicious little shit I'd ever dealt with. She actually believed that her father would be in trouble for enforcing a dress code. I told her to get out of my office, and that I would see her again in the future, probably in handcuffs."

Cheryl D. 37
probation officer

"My daughter gave me a lesson in child psychology when I caught her watching TV instead of doing her homework—for about the fifteenth time. I asked her to explain why she chose to watch TV rather than doing what I told her to. She rolled her eyes at me like I was an idiot and said 'Don't you get it, Mom?—because it's easier.' I quit bugging her about her homework and chores, and I quit doing the laundry and cooking, and when she needed a ride I faked a headache. She got fed up and yelled at me about not doing anything, so I told her I gave up on motherhood. She was flabbergasted, and asked *'Why?'* I said 'Because it's easier.' She's still a snotty brat, but her grades are up."

Judy G. 35
retail sales

"There's only one way to have good kids—learn what makes a good man, find one and marry him. Be faithful and treat him like a king, and allow his natural logic to help make the important decisions. And tell your mother to mind her own business."

Valerie N. 41
work-at-home mom

"I'm amazed at people who want to take guns away from everyone because a few crazies get ahold of one. Why don't they take away an idiot's ability to procreate?—that causes more suffering than guns. It's my job to see young girls through their labor and delivery, and I'm supposed to be as happy for them as I am for a married couple who actually *have* the ability to love and feed a newborn. I want to strangle these young girls—and their unemployed boyfriends—especially when they're rude to the staff, like we're their incompetent servants."

Linda O. 38
nurse, labor & delivery

"Step-parenting should be against the law. A woman who marries a man before her kids are grown and gone is treating *her* loneliness—not her kids'. Her brothers or her father could help provide male influence, and double her parenting efforts. Are kids supposed to be relieved and happy their mother moved a stranger into her bed because she was lonely? Kids will never submit to a stepparent, and there will be constant tension and resistance."

Deede E. 23
student/stepchild

"I will *never* have children—they're dangerous. Girls in middle school actually plot with each other about overthrowing their parents' authority, and one of their tactics is to falsely accuse their parents of sexual molestation. It happens all the time, and there are parents in prison just because they said 'no' to their daughters. I refuse to be alone with a student because I don't want to give them the opportunity to invent lies about me."

Mackenzie T. 27
middle-school teacher

"We lost control of our son when he was fifteen—his drug abuse was getting worse every day. We found a rehab program in Utah that had an impressive success rate, but my son wouldn't go. When we called them for help they said his unwillingness wouldn't be a problem. Two huge men burst into his room at 3:00 AM and dragged him to their van in handcuffs. He was kicking and screaming, but it didn't do any good. They took him to a campsite in the middle of nowhere and told him he could leave anytime, but it was a seven-day hike if the bears didn't eat him. They kept him for three months and he was a completely different person when he came home. After he graduated from high school he joined the Marines. The program cost $58,000 and it was worth every penny."

Jamie J. 42
business owner

"There's a trend among women who dislike their husbands. They treat their kids as friends to fill that void that all man-haters have. Mothers stunt their children's growth with guilt to keep them around longer—especially sons. These mothers need to grow up and have adult relationships with their husbands. Kids are born with a built-in divorce that allows them to become adults, and mothers should do everything they can to prepare them for it. A marriage is the opposite and should *not* include a divorce. Women are screwing up their own families."

Aileen I. 47
cosmetic sales

"I hate beauty pageants—that is *not* parenting. My niece is only six, and my sister is destroying her little mind by making her believe she's the most beautiful little girl in the world. She asked me 'Auntie, do you think I'm pretty?' My sister has become addicted to it and she hates the other mothers and their daughters with a passion. I'm serious—she needs professional help. I can't talk to her about it because she starts screaming at me and accusing me of being jealous of my niece. I don't know how, but they brainwashed her."

Shawn C. 25
jewelry sales associate

"My best friend was married with three kids, and her youngest was three years old. She ran off with her college professor and left the 3-year-old with her husband. She told me she did it to keep him busy so he wouldn't look for her. I was blown away! Mothers are not supposed to give up their kids. I thought I knew her better."

Gloria H. 34
charter pilot

"My daughter died when she was twenty-eight years old. She was a heroin addict, and she started taking drugs when she was twelve. My second husband was an alcoholic with two older sons who drank and did drugs. They introduced my daughter to drugs in my own house. When my son was just sixteen his stepdad forced him off my property, and I just stood there. Everyone at work told me it wasn't my fault, but it was."

Eleanor B. 60
office worker

"Why do so many middle-aged women still have their sons living with them? I know three divorced women whose sons have *never* left home. None of these women can get a second date with anyone because there's already a man in the house. Their sons hardly ever work. One woman's son stole her keys and wrecked her car, and he doesn't even have a license to drive—at twenty-nine! These adult sons still throw tantrums and punch holes in the walls when they don't get their way. Maybe she's found a twisted replacement for a relationship with a real man—who knows?"

Loretta S. 51
physical-education teacher

"The one thing every man should know before he agrees to father children is that women will always own the children. I don't mean legally, but emotionally. Children can disown a father, but never a mother, no matter how mean and vindictive she is. It's human nature, and a man will always lose any battle fought over children. Sorry, but it's true."

Haley W. 52
grocery clerk

"I had zero impact on my daughters after they turned thirteen. They ignored my rules and treated me like the enemy. Now they're adult women with no skills whatsoever. They can't cook, keep a job, or budget money. After years of partying and having sex with anybody and everybody, they want to get married so they don't starve. They've both asked me if they could move back home and I told them 'Hell, no!' My parenting skills were just fine. *They* decided to ruin their lives—not me."

Brenda F. 49
property manager

"Young girls are mistaking puberty for a signal to make babies. You would think we'd be more civilized by now. No place to live, no husband, no job—*yeah*, let's get knocked-up!"

Carma R. 31
county health department

"You know about those jelly bracelets, right?—different colors have different meanings? Our kids are sending secret messages with them, and bragging to each other about what they've done. There are colors that advertise the kind of sexual experiences they've had—or are *willing* to have. The meanings vary in different areas, and I'm not sure I know what they are. To think my daughter could buy a cheap plastic bracelet in a color that tells boys she'll take it in the ass!—*What the hell am I supposed to do about that?!*"

Eve M. 39
concerned parent

"I was at war with my parents since I was fifteen years old. Mom was the tyrant in my family. I never argued with her because I was scared to death of her. I fought her by hooking up with a long-haired guy who rode a motorcycle, then an alcoholic, and then a black guy. I made her suffer without saying a word."

Jules L. 30
roadie

"I always felt different because I didn't look anything like my three sisters, and I was for sure treated differently. When I was eighteen years old my grandma told me that my dad wasn't my real dad—I was adopted. I confronted my mom, and she threw a frying pan at me and locked herself in her bedroom. I was forty years old before I found my real father and my half-brother and sister. I thought it would help me to understand and feel better about it, but I just felt even more ripped-off. It was too late—they tried to love me, but I was from another time and it was awkward for them. My mom was horrified at the thought of everyone knowing she'd been an unwed mother forty-some years ago. She wanted a different history, and for decades she involved everyone around her in a lie, trying to make it happen."

Renata P. 48
retail store owner

18 mothers

"I grew up despising my mother's behavior and I swore I would never be like her. I caught myself ordering the kids around before school the other day, and I heard my mother's voice coming from *me!* My god, I sounded just like her. How do mothers do it? I might need professional help."
    Kinley W. 34
    speech therapist

"Mothers are the apex predators of women in our world. A woman doesn't realize her full potential until she gives birth, and then she has the ultimate control. Mothers can make their kids fat or skinny, and well-adjusted or totally screwed-up. How the kid turns out depends on how her mother treats her, and how much leftover hate she has for her own mother. We're at the mercy of the womb until we die—and maybe longer."
    Madison M. 41
    social worker

"Nobody's approval is more satisfying than your mother's. Trying to please your mother is above and beyond everything. It will never happen, but we still try."
    Ann F. 32
    ticket sales

"The worst wives and mothers in the world are women who are still controlled by their mothers, and that's the majority of them."
Zelda J. 67
retired bookkeeper

"My mom didn't like my husband because he had a mind of his own and didn't hesitate to share his opposing thoughts with her. She was used to being obeyed, and when he came along she made up her mind that he didn't belong. I had always lived under her thumb until I married him, but she accused *him* of controlling my mind. She knew she couldn't break him down so she started in on me. It took her over a year to break me, but she finally caused enough grief in my house that we got divorced. I didn't see what she was doing until it was too late. I was devastated by the divorce and her only words of comfort were 'You're better off without him,' and then she ignored me. She called me every day when I was married, but since the divorce I might hear from her once a month. Thanks, Mom."
Robin Q. 37
bridal consultant

"I still feel like a little kid in trouble when I talk to my mom. Why can't I grow up?"
Bertha S. 52
mortician

"My brother got sole custody of his daughter when she was six years old because her mother was using drugs. My brother took her to court to force her into a drug test, but she signed over custody instead. For seven years she never called or sent her daughter a birthday card. My brother was the best father I've ever seen—it's like he was born to be a parent. When my niece was thirteen she wanted to see her mother for the first time in all those years, so my brother let her spend the weekend with her under supervision. After just one visit my niece turned on my brother and she was totally out-of-control. He pleaded and fought with her for the next two years, and finally gave in and sent her to live with her mother. My niece started drinking and using drugs with her mother, and she posted all of it online. When my brother saw it he almost died. The drug-addict mother won."
Collette K. 46
salon owner

"My mom has full-blown Narcissistic Personality Disorder and I was raised to be just like her. You really ought to read about it because it will help you understand most of the problems you've ever had with women. I'm forty-five years old, and looking back, I never made a single decision on my own—my mother made them for me. I hate it, but it's too late for me to change. I'm a *mom-zombie*—that's what I call women who can't break free from their mother's control, and there are a lot of us."

Evie L. 45
physical therapy coordinator

"My younger brother and I always believed we had the same father. My dad always denied it, and Mom called him a deadbeat father. She had everybody in the family hating him, including me. Finally, when my little brother was twenty-eight he called my dad and asked him to have a DNA test. He agreed, and he even paid for it. When Mom found out she went crazy. It proved that my dad wasn't his real father, but she denied it for weeks. She even accused my dad of hacking into the DNA lab's database because he knows how to fix computers. My dad's girlfriend sent the test results to all my mom's family and friends and *Oh, my god!* My little brother backed my mom into a corner and demanded the truth. She was tired of lying, and said 'Let me think about it.' Long story short, she told my brother who his real father was, and then he had a DNA test that proved it. Apparently, Mom had found herself backstage at some rodeo concert and hooked up with this drummer. She said she drank a couple of beers and the rest was a blur—*Yeah, right!* My little brother finally has a really cool dad. They're close, and they both play drums. Mom's social page is private now."

Macy C. 36
bank executive

"My dad raised me because my mother was a flake. I started getting cramps when I was twelve so he got books about menstruation from the library, and he had heart-to-heart talks with me about being a woman. When I was thirteen I came out of the bathroom in shock and told him I had started. I didn't have anybody else to tell. I swear to God, he gave me a high-five and said 'Congratulations!'"

Halee H. 21
waitress

"When I started my period I thought I was dying. Mom never warned me about it. I went to the bathroom and my panties were soaked with blood, and I screamed for her. When she saw the blood she reached under the sink and said 'Here's a pad,' and she walked away. I realized later that it should have been an important rite of passage into womanhood, but she made me feel like I had done something wrong. When *my* daughter started I threw a party with a cake and invited all her girlfriends. I made her feel like a young woman—the young woman I could never be."

Marguerite F. 50
massage therapist

"We warn men to look at the mother if they want to know what a woman is really like, but they just don't listen. They give women too much credit for having a mind of their own, when the mother is the one in control. Men think we're warning them about how their fiancée will look, but really it's how they will act."

Kimberley R. 58
management

"The only way I got attention from my mom was to mix her a drink. At ten years old I made a killer whiskey sour."

Marlene P. 52
business consultant

"My mom wanted me to be ugly. She wears her hair really short and she dyes it fire-engine red. For years I wore my hair the same way. I would fight with anybody who tried to tell me I looked like my mom, but they were right. My boyfriend thought my natural color was beautiful so I decided to grow it out for him. When I cut off the last of the red, my mom reached up and grabbed a handful of my hair and said 'What are we going to do with this mop?' Now my hair goes down to my bra strap, and it's beautiful—I get compliments all the time. I don't understand why my mom wants me to look like her."

Cindy Y. 41
county employee

"When I finally introduced my fiancé to my mother, she treated him like he was a leper. She invited us in and she sat in the middle of the eight-foot-long couch. My fiancé had to remind me later that I sat on the floor at her feet, looking up at her in submission. I argued with him at first, but he was right. My mother scares the shit out of me. I was groveling at her feet for permission to even have a boyfriend, let alone a fiancé. He was very polite to her, he was gorgeous, and he owned his own business and drove a new car. But she told me he wasn't good enough for me after spending only thirty minutes with him. She disapproved, and we never got married. Now *that's* control!"

Beverley T. 34
schoolteacher

"When I was thirty-two I worked for a big electronics company that offered incentives for the best sales. I won a trip to Cancun, Mexico and I invited my mom to go with me. We were in Mexico for nine days and we spent the whole time eating, drinking, and shopping. I felt like a little girl with her standing next to me—I actually cowered. I kept my hands in my pockets so I wouldn't break anything, and I expected to be chastised for being so clumsy. Our trip made me realize that she had never let me grow up, and I started wondering how that had affected the other parts of my life. I'm still her little girl. Hold me!"

Irene H. 56
real estate investor

"So what if our mothers fucked us up? *Big fucking deal!* Our mothers were fucked-up by their mothers, who were fucked-up by their mothers, alright? The problem isn't that our mothers molded us into what we are—the problem is with women who refuse to make themselves into what *they* want to be. I know it's a cycle, but it can be broken—I did it. I know what it's like to have a mother controlling every square inch of your life. I decided to be my own person, and I have a good husband and well-adjusted kids who are too terrified of me to do anything wrong—they know I'll fucking kill them. These whiny fucking women who tell each other how to live should grow a pair of their own."

Berta D. 38
lingerie store manager

"No matter what my mother does—and she's done some really bad stuff—I always say 'But she's still my mother'. I can't count the people who have ditched me for saying that."

Clara L. 21
horse wrangler

"Man-haters can't help but teach their daughters the same thing. Hate can't keep its mouth shut."

Joan Y. 30
retail sales

"I was visiting with my mom and she asked me how much money my husband made. I told her and she got really angry. She called me a liar and said nobody as young as my husband could make that much. He was in construction and he made more than my dad, and it pissed her off. She told me there's no way my husband could make two-and-a-half times as much as my father because my father had a college degree. She made me leave and threatened to disown me if I ever talked about it again."

Darcy B. 28
housewife

"Why does a mother get so much credit for just giving birth? For shit's sake, there are mothers in prison for killing their husbands and their kids—does anybody read the news? My mother tortured me because I ruined her life by being born. I've heard the story about how long she was in labor at least a million times. The first time she told the story she was in labor for twenty-four hours, and every time after that she added twelve hours to it. The last time I heard it I think she was in labor for six months, and it was all my fault! There are good mothers and bad mothers. It's up to the kids to figure out which kind they have, and live their lives accordingly."

Megan H. 21
student

"My mother ended my marriage, and I let her. My husband was really good to me, but I couldn't shit without asking my mother. Looking back, I'm amazed he stayed with me as long as he did. I wasn't married to *him*—I was married to my mother. It's sick, I know, but it's true."

Donna P. 37
store manager

"My mother can still cripple me with just a look. She's the boss, and I'm her slave."

Abby V. 39
medical supply sales

"Do you want to know how spineless I am? I invited my dad to visit, but with the condition that my mom could never know I saw him. I was terrified she would find out that I wanted to see my father. I asked him to meet me at a place where Mom wouldn't catch us together. He said he didn't want to see me if I was that ashamed of him. Can you believe I actually told him that?"

Stacey R. 35
legal secretary

"Since I was seventeen, three of my boyfriends told me that my mother tried to seduce them. I didn't want to believe it so I broke up with them. When my husband said she tried to seduce *him* I got so mad I gave him a black eye. I knew he wasn't lying, but I couldn't face my mother about it. I can fight a man, but I can't even talk to my mother."

Erica T. 25
business administrator

"I fucked at least a hundred men before I figured out that my mother doesn't approve of *any* man. I was looking for somebody my mom would approve of, but I didn't know it could never happen. Look what I did to myself."

Sarah B. 46
public transportation

"Our mothers are enemies when it comes to finding a good man. We can't be in a happy relationship with a man unless we completely disown our mothers, and that really hurts. Men don't get this at all."

Stacy Q. 26
dispatcher

"Mothers corrupt daughters, but mothers with money corrupt daughters absolutely. Don't ever forget that."

Jill H. 68
retired military

19 abuse & control

"I've never hit my husband and he's never hit me. I believe if you're going to hit a man, you'd better be ready to get hit back. We always bitch about not being treated as equals—hit a man and we'll see how equal we are. And don't call the police on him if he wins the fistfight that you started."
Yvonne G. 41
parking attendant

"I beat the shit out of my husband all the time. I blacked both his eyes, broke a beer bottle over his head, and once I even threw a knife at him, but it missed. He won't lay a hand on me. He knows better."
Holly V. 27
auto transport

"I *wanted* my husband to hit me. I was having an affair and he had no idea. I felt so guilty, but I couldn't tell him and break his heart. I tried to tell him a thousand times, but it always stuck in my throat. I'd start a fight and try to get him to react so I could leave him for hitting me, instead of having him leave me for adultery. He never would hit me—he just thought I had PMS really bad."
Amber D. 26
cocktail waitress

"When it comes to physical abuse I agree with my grandma. The first time he hits you it's his fault—every time after that is your fault. If my husband ever hit me, I would leave for good. But I don't have to worry about it because I took my time finding a good man from a good family that doesn't have a history of violence. Most women don't do that."

Maggie E. 27
jewelry sales

"I left my husband after two years because I never really wanted to be married. I finally got pregnant and qualified for welfare, so I bolted. When I moved back in with my parents I had to make up a quick story about why I left, so I told my mom that my husband had beat me for the whole two years. She looked me right in the eye and said 'Bullshit!' She knew him better than that, and obviously she could still tell when I was lying. I caved in and told her I couldn't handle the responsibility and the boredom. She just sighed, and never mentioned it again. I liked the lie better."

Penny T. 26
welfare recipient

"I'm at the women's shelter every couple of months. I know everybody there. When my old man gets too full of himself I get him all riled up and I get him to smack me, and off he goes to jail. It's kind of like a time-out for big boys. He's been to more court-ordered anger management classes than the dude that teaches it."

Rhianna J. 31
unemployed

"I work the graveyard shift at the shelter for abused women—I'm an intake counselor. It's just a revolving door for the same group of angry, bored women who are addicted to melodrama. Their biggest problem is they don't even like men. They sit around and brag about their last fight and how pitiful their men look sitting in the back of a police car—and they laugh about it! When I'm conducting the intake they're all helpless and victimized, but when they get together with the other women they compare notes about how to push a man's buttons and get him to hit you. I overheard one of them boasting that she could get *any* man to hit her. She was instructing the others and she said 'If you verbally poke him in the chest enough, he *will* hit you.' We refer to it as the 'dance' with men to get attention and exercise control. Once in a great while we get a genuine victim of unsolicited abuse, and the other women try to recruit her into thinking their way. I constantly have to remind the drama queens that *I'm* the counselor and they need to keep their mouths shut. I applied for this job hoping to help others, but they don't need help. This is the life they choose and they aren't going to give it up. It's the most frustrating job I've ever had."

Maya R. 37
counselor

"Why do women look away if their own children are being abused in the home? It doesn't even have to be the children's father—it could be her boyfriend and she still looks away. But let someone try to make her do something she doesn't want to do, and the police are on their way. Is it just me, or do we have a double standard here?"

Lorene N. 48
crisis-line counselor

"Why did he hit her? Why did she get raped? That's what people *should* be asking. Women used to have skills that protected them from abuse. Do you think women running around half-naked might have something to do with at least a rape or two? How about women who are so mouthy that even other women slap the shit out of them? Could that cause a man to smack his wife? You're goddamn right it could, but everybody wants to sensationalize the event and ignore the cause. They get more attention being a victim than a wise woman."

Grace U. 57
real estate agent

"I think men are far more sympathetic than women toward other women who've been raped. The first thing I want to know is what the circumstances were. If she was in a situation she knew could be dangerous, I have *no* sympathy. Some women seem to believe that their rights are so sacred that no man would dare violate them. That's a pretty naive way to think. A woman can taunt most men with sexual innuendo and racy outfits that show more skin than most lingerie does, and even then she's usually safe in most places. But someday she'll cross paths with a rapist."

Gloria K. 45
home loan officer

"If women would quit accusing men of rape when it really didn't happen, maybe they would catch the real rapists. The courts and jails are full of men who just made some vindictive woman mad. My own sister did it. She would get so angry at her husband she would throw stuff at him—I mean big stuff like the iron. She really needed some anger-management classes. One time they were arguing and my brother-in-law wouldn't listen to her, so she bashed her own face into the door frame and cut her eyebrow wide open. Then she called 911 and told them he pushed her and raped her. He went to jail and was convicted of domestic violence and rape, and they confiscated his gun collection. My sister thinks it's funny that he's now a registered sex offender and can't ever buy a gun again. No, they're not together anymore."

Yolanda F. 33
fabric store owner

"One of the girls at work is telling everybody that her husband raped her, and she filed charges against him. I guess he even spent a night in jail. What a crock of shit! Her husband is twenty-eight and he's just a walking hormone—what does she expect? She said they fucked like rabbits before they got married, and she used to tell us how erotic it was to tie each other up. Now he's a rapist?—*Women!* Unbridled sex was how she got him to marry her, and just because she has a headache she wants to cut him off. How about a nice quick hand-job to help him sleep? Just wait—it won't be long before she's griping about him being unfaithful. Exerting control through melodrama is all that drives some women, and they encourage each other to do it."

Helen D. 46
bank teller

"I don't feel the least bit sorry for these tramps who get 'raped.' If they dress like a prostitute and act like a prostitute, they should expect to be treated like one. Some of them act like it's a horrible crime when a girl goes to a bar in stilettos, ass and boobs hanging out, drinks herself into a stupor, and then says she was raped—I don't think so. They go looking for trouble, and they find it—no, they *make* the trouble. They get hammered and they're rubbing their bare tits all over everybody, begging to be noticed. They'll get some poor guy all worked-up just because they can, and then change their mind in the morning. The word 'rape' has been worn out by some sorry-ass women who deserved what they got—and it *wasn't* rape. The few women who are attacked and raped for real, who didn't ask for it, are lost in a crowd of the ones who did. Then they're all herded through the system like cattle and nobody can tell the difference. Women have each other to blame for the lack of respect we get over this issue."

Clancy C. 37
singer

"What exactly *is* rape anyway? If I go to a party and get drunk and wake up with a guy I don't know, was I raped? If I'm eighteen years old and I go to Mexico to party in the streets and end up pregnant or dead, was I violated? The answer is no, and no! If you go swimming with sharks, you can't blame the one that ate you. Girls who create these situations want to cry foul and get attention for what happened to them, and they want to make someone else pay for it. Why not punish these idiot women for the stupid choices they made? It just make us all look irresponsible and dumb."

Carmen Z. 32
legal secretary

"Cry wolf or cry rape—same thing. A friend of mine got in a fight with her husband and she jumped out of the car forty miles from home. She hid in an alley until he gave up looking for her, and then she started hitchhiking home. Some guy picked her up, they bought some beer and they ended up at a park where they did the dirty deed. The guy drops her off at home and she walks in the house with weeds in her hair and smelling like beer. Her husband went crazy, so she said she'd been raped. Her husband called the cops and she gave them the guy's first name and a description of his car. They took her to the hospital and did a rape kit on her. You're not going to believe this—I knew the guy! I went to high school with him. He's a womanizer, but he's not a rapist. Friends close to him told me what happened when he got home. He went straight to the shower and then sat in his recliner where his wife brought him dinner. While he was eating, the cops knocked on his door and arrested him for rape. He finally beat the charges because my friend's story kept changing, but when he got out of jail his wife was gone."

Spring A. 36
truck driver

"I think there's a lot of crying 'wolf' out there, but I do work with a girl who was truly a victim. She's only twenty-five and the sweetest, most wholesome girl I ever met. Her husband left her and her baby for his old girlfriend, and it wiped her out. For a year she didn't do anything but work and take care of her daughter. The girls at work kept trying to get her go out with them, but she wasn't the partying type. They finally made her feel so bad that she agreed to go out for one drink. Her mom dropped her off at the lounge, but when she went back to pick her up, she was gone. A highway patrolman found her at five o'clock the next morning, fifteen miles from town on a deserted road, stark naked. She didn't know where she was or how she got there. She'd been drugged and raped multiple times. We learned that there are two bartenders in town who were willing to spike someone's drink for fifty bucks."

Judith A. 43
office manager

"There just isn't enough manpower to separate the false accusations from actual child abuse. Since the early '80s a lot of real victims have slipped through the cracks because of it. The cases that do get prosecuted only make it more attractive to women intent on upsetting a father's visitation. I know for a fact that we've put innocent men in jail, and equally as tragic are the children who will never see their fathers again. Remember, hell hath no fury…"

Blanca G. 47
legal stuff ("close enough")

"I'd be afraid to claim that I was abused—as a child *or* as an adult. It's become the universal excuse for everything from shoplifting to murdering your children. I don't want to be associated with a bunch of women who think they don't have to honor their marriage vows because they were potty-trained too soon."

Blake L. 29
county records

"My sister went to jail and my 13-year-old niece moved in with us. She was already kind of mixed-up, but I thought we would be a good influence on her. The first week she was there I came home from work and found my husband waiting for me a block from our house. He was pale, and he told me he was walking down the hallway and my niece blocked his way, wrapped her arms around him and tried to kiss him—tongue and all. I got mad at him for lying! I didn't want to believe him, but I remembered how my mom covered it up when I got molested at twelve years old. Now I know how my mom felt. I wanted to crawl in a hole and hide. My husband wasn't lying, and my niece admitted everything after I called her on it. I could have handled a threat from outside the family better than one from inside. I immediately moved my niece out of the house and I started apologizing to my husband. He was hurt to the core that I hadn't believed him, but he finally forgave me."

Jennifer Y. 31
emergency room nurse

"Oh, please!—do you know how many women were molested as girls? I was molested by a neighbor for years, but I grew up and realized that as an adult *I* was now in charge of who touched me. I could have blamed my mother for not watching me closely enough, but I didn't. I never wanted to go on TV or write a book about how screwed-up I am. I choose to live in the now, not the past. I got a lot of inspiration from a story about men who were railroaded by crooked prosecutors and spent ten, twenty, or thirty years in prison for things they hadn't done. When they were released not one of them was bitter about it, and they were intent on living for today. A lot of psychologists made a ton of money popularizing something women have dealt with since the beginning of time. Our innocence has value, but so does a car. Anything of value is at risk of being taken away. It's the reality of human nature. Get a grip, and live your life."

Bonnie H. 63
retail manager

"If a man comes into my bar for a drink and there's a girl with an I.D. that says she's twenty-five years old—and she looks every bit of twenty-five—and he ends up in bed with her but she's really only seventeen, what the hell did he do wrong? I don't think that should be called statutory rape, but one of my customers went to jail for just that. The judge said a 17-year-old girl wasn't capable of making those kinds of decisions, but *he* was. What the fuck?—*Over!*"

Vi L. 48
bar owner

"We can't control ourselves, but we can control men. We'll try to get them to hit us, and then pretend we have no control at all. We like the power trip of playing the victim, and we love the attention when the cops take revealing photos of our bruises. It's all part of the game."
Honey B. 36
liquor store clerk

"My boyfriend used to freak out when I would drive alone at three o'clock in the morning to see him. It was a hundred-mile trip and half of it was in the middle of nowhere. No cell service—nothing. He did it all the time, but he was worried that I might break down and be assaulted by some prowling rapist. I thought he was being sexist and controlling, until he offered to take me to the rape crisis center to see how many men were in the stirrups having a rape exam done—good point. He really *was* trying to protect me, so I married him!"
Christina Y. 25
dental lab technician

20 regrets

"I repeated it over and over in my head when I was younger—'The past is the past.' Every time I woke up naked and hung-over and couldn't remember the night before, I thought to myself 'The past is the past.' I used to say it out loud in the shower, trying to wash it off. Well, you know what?—the past matters. I tried to convince myself that it shouldn't matter to a man who really loved me, but it has affected me way more that it could possibly affect a man. I'm the one who lived it. *Of course* a man can overlook my past—he doesn't have to carry it around all day."

May K. 37
retail sales

"I regret my twenties. All the guys were after me and I just assumed it was because I was thinner and prettier than my friends. I was the last one to know I had a reputation. I thought I was rewarding the guys I dated by sleeping with them. Sometimes I wondered why they never asked me out a second time, but I had so many other offers that I didn't dwell on it. I was in my thirties and still single before I finally got a clue, but it was too late. You could find my phone number on a lot of restroom walls by then. I moved out-of-state, and my husband doesn't know what I used to be."

Alicia D. 41
event planner

"This guy would come to my work and he always got in line at my check-stand, even if it was the longest line. He would buy a few little things and he'd come back later and say he'd forgotten something. He was cute and really funny, and I started looking for him after a while. After about two months he finally got up the nerve to ask me out. I stiffened right up and I told him 'I'm fat, and I have two kids.' That's all I said, and I never saw him again. What was I thinking? I'm such a dumbshit! I got laid-off three weeks later, and I miss *him* more than I miss my job. I never even knew his last name."

Joelle T. 36
grocery clerk

"Ever since we first met, my husband would always open the car door for me. He'd shut off the car, get out and walk around to my side, and open my door. Strange women in parking lots would stop and tell us how sweet and nice it was to see such respect. This one woman even pointed us out to her husband as they were walking by, and then punched him in the arm. One day I was grouchy and felt like arguing. I don't even remember what I was mad about—probably something to do with my mother, but I took it out on my husband. I was ranting and raving, but he didn't want to fight. I just wanted to attack something so I attacked his chivalry. I told him I didn't like him opening my door for me. He was shocked, and he apologized and promised it wouldn't happen again. After I calmed down I didn't give it a second thought. The next time we went somewhere my husband got out of the car and I waited for my door to open—but it didn't. I looked back and saw my husband walking off without me. I was crushed, but I'd asked for it. He hasn't opened my door since."

Frankie A. 35
bookkeeper

"When I was in college I ran into this guy I had known from high school. We were both divorced and older than most of the students, so we hung out together. He'd stay late to meet me after my last class and walk me to my car. It was so cool, like we were in high school again. He asked me out to dinner, but he wouldn't tell me where we were going. I asked him what I should wear and he said 'your nicest dress.' I was giddy. We were both full-time students and

I knew he was stretching his budget to make me feel special. He told me to meet him at the airport so I assumed he was taking me to the restaurant there, which was pretty fancy. I parked next to his car, and he opened my door and offered me his arm. I felt like Cinderella! He walked me to this locked gate where the airplanes were parked and punched in a code. The gate opened, and I freaked out. I just knew we were going to get arrested. We walked up to this airplane, and he pulled out a key and opened the door—*Holy shit!* He buckled me in and started the engine, and the next thing I knew we were flying up the coast at night. The view was spectacular. We landed a hundred miles from home, and a taxi took us to the coolest restaurant I'd ever seen. When we got back he walked me to my car and kissed me. The next day I told the girls in my first class about my date, and they all wanted to meet him. He was waiting for me outside and twenty girls swarmed around him—I couldn't believe it. They were all saying 'Take me next, take me,' like he was some kind of carnival ride. He turned beet-red and he looked at me like 'Help!' I just walked away and left him with his fans. I was pissed-off at him for my own jealousy. I started avoiding him, and he finally got the message. It still makes me mad to talk about it."

Ladonna G. 32
retail sales

"I was divorced and I hadn't dated for eighteen years. I met this gorgeous man and I wanted him to notice me in the worst way. I had forgotten how to get a man's attention, and I asked my single friends what to do—I can't believe I'm telling you this. So my friends tell me that guys like women to be more aggressive, and I need to use my imagination. So I buy a box of condoms, and I write my phone number on the box and put it in a brown paper bag—this is so embarrassing. I knock on his door, and when he answers I hand him the bag and *run away!*—I mean I *ran* to my car and drove off without a word. He came over the next day and ended up spending the night with me, and I made him breakfast in the morning. We were both so bashful we hardly talked. All he said was 'I have to admit, that's a first for me.' He kissed me goodbye, and I never heard from him again."

Judy T. 41
manicurist

"Every woman has at least one very dark secret spinning around in her head. If you doubt it—well, you're just stupid. Attention is intoxicating, and when a girl goes through puberty the attention she attracts is impossible to ignore because it's the first taste of her power over men."
   Stella A. 57
   probation officer

"On our first anniversary my husband surprised me and took me to a super-elegant restaurant. He had always been nervous in crowded public places, so I was amazed that he wanted to do it. But his shyness was one of the things I fell in love with in the first place. I knew he wouldn't stray because strange women made him almost faint. When the band started playing in the lounge I wanted to dance. Of course I knew from the start that he didn't dance, but I was a spoiled little brat and I wanted my way. I kept nagging him to dance, but he just couldn't do it. So I got up and went to the lounge, and asked a stranger to dance. My husband could see us from the table and he just watched. I ruined the whole night, and hurt him worse than I knew. I made one of his most attractive traits into something to feel bad about. From then on he felt like he wasn't good enough for me. There are some things you can't undo, but *God*, I wish I hadn't done that!"
   Andi V. 31
   home healthcare

"I should have gone to college. My sister and brother both did, and my parents tried to get me to go, but I was too busy partying. My high-school friends all faded away and I never saw them in the clubs. Everybody said the past doesn't matter, and I believed that horseshit! Not only does your sexual past matter, but your educational past matters, too. It decides what kind of person you're you'll end up with. My 20-year class reunion committee called and asked me to help contact the other people from my graduating class. I was excited to see all my old boyfriends because I was pretty sure I was still better-looking than most of the girls from high school. I borrowed money from my mom to buy a new outfit for the dance. When I started calling people I ended up talking with women, mostly. Some of them were my classmates, but quite a few others were wives of my old boyfriends. I was getting details for a class-reunion book, and just about everyone had college degrees or successful businesses. They had nice kids, nice houses and nice cars, and I drove to work in the old beater my grandma gave me. I'm divorced, and I work the graveyard shift at a convenience store. I finished calling everyone, and I took the new outfit back to the store and changed my phone number. I worked an extra shift on the night of the dance."

Evelyn B. 43
clerk

"If I had it to do over I would stay a virgin until I was forty. I used to have sex with strangers like most people shake hands. I'm amazed that I haven't died from AIDS, or at the hands of some lowlife I banged. I think about what I've done every single day. There's no amount of therapy that can erase the memory of all the random guys I slept with, and that's not healthy. I finally bought a vibrator and gave up men altogether. The last few times I had sex, I saw the faces of all the men I had 'entertained,' and it finally ruined the experience. I'll tell you something else—women don't forget anything. They remember every wrong they've ever done."

Kay I. 51
certified public accountant

"I woke up on the floor stuck between a bed and a wall. My clothes were gone and my skin looked like a glazed doughnut. I was completely alone in a strange house. I remembered going to a party and drinking vodka straight from the bottle—big mistake. I found my shorts in the kitchen and my blouse on the back patio. I got dressed and ran barefoot to a gas station to find out where I was, which turned out to be over a hundred miles from home. My purse was gone and I didn't know where my car was, so I made a collect call to my girlfriend. She was too hung-over to drive. I waited there for seven hours before she picked me up, and I had to have an abortion. I can't get it out of my mind."

Sharr L. 24
college student

"I was sitting in the clinic in a paper gown waiting for my fourth abortion. When you're too drunk to think about birth control, you're too drunk to have sex. I remember thinking I really should do something about it. I didn't know who any of the fathers were."

Wanda H. 35
court clerk

"I started a new job and there were men everywhere. They acted like they had never seen a woman before, and they all wanted to talk to me. I was flattered that they thought I was so interesting and attractive. In eight months I slept with five different guys from work. I just wrote it off to not finding the right one yet. I was so stupid! One of the girls finally took me aside and told me that everyone in the office knew what I'd been doing, and that three of the men were married—they just didn't wear their wedding rings at work. They described me as having been 'passed around,' and I wasn't the first new girl to do it. I quit the next day."
Lila N. 24
unemployed

"There are two things that will make a girl take her clothes off in public—getting really drunk, and being in front of a camera. On Friday after work my friends and I would pile in a car to go hit the bars in a town two hours away. We rented a motel room so we could get all fixed-up and have a place to bring the guys. We'd drag them over there and fuck them, and then wash up and go back to the bar. It was like a marathon. We could usually do three guys in a night. We never paid for drinks, because we dressed like hookers. One night they were shooting video of everybody dancing. I was pretty wasted and when I saw the camera I just took my top off. I know why those girls on spring break pull their shirts up—you just can't help it. I wanted to be the center of attention. A bouncer and a cocktail waitress grabbed me and shoved me out the door. They threw my top at me and yelled 'Don't come back!' I can still hear that. I waited outside for my friends, and I had time to think. I've been thinking about it ever since—that was *me* that did that shit."
Rae V. 28
real estate developer

"I was dirt-poor until my parents died and I inherited some money. I took my boyfriend to Hawaii and we got in a fight, so I left him there. I highly recommend leaving someone on an island—it's way better than murdering him. It took him five months to find his way back to the mainland, and I spent them looking up old boyfriends and paying for their tickets to come and have their way with me. When my boyfriend came back we made up and it was business-as-usual. But I woke up one morning and felt like my pussy was on fire. My boyfriend said it looked like someone had burned me with a cigar all over down there. I raced to the doctor and he diagnosed me with genital herpes. I was mortified. He started me on medication that made me sick, and he told us to use condoms from then on. I was hoping I hadn't infected my boyfriend, but about a month later his scrotum was covered with oozing, bleeding sores. That ended it, and I've been alone ever since."

Joanne J. 55
retired

"I learned the hard way that I'm one of those people who just can't drink. I came to, face-down on a toilet in a men's-room stall with my pants around my ankles. There were men with cell phones taking pictures of me. Someone finally helped me to my feet and pulled my pants up. That night was the last time I drank alcohol."

Yoly F. 34
hairstylist

"I had an abortion when I was seventeen because I didn't want my mother to know I was sleeping with my boyfriend. She had threatened that if I got pregnant, she wouldn't pay for college. I have a daughter now, and every time I look at her I see the face of the one I killed."

Ondine P. 26
daycare worker

"My husband left me after fifteen years of marriage, and if I wasn't at work I was sitting at home crying. My friends tried for months to get me out of the house, but I fought them off. I wanted to grieve. They finally convinced me to go with them on a trip to Tijuana to have some fun. The last thing I remembered was a cantina on the street where they pour tequila from the bottle straight into your mouth. I must have had too many because I lost all control and all memory of what happened, and it was bad. I woke up four days later at a truck stop in Memphis, Tennessee in the sleeper of a big diesel truck. I was naked except for the racing stickers on my belly. The driver must have been in the restaurant. I rummaged around and found some clothes, and I walked to a pay phone. I called my friend and she wired me the money to get home. She had been frantic for days—I had gone to the bathroom at the cantina, and that was the last she saw of me. I'm still grieving."

Toni H. 46
secondhand book vendor

"Three of my friends and I saved our money and went to Las Vegas for the first time. It was summertime and it was really hot, so we dressed for the heat. It was like a hundred degrees at midnight and we weren't wearing much. We gambled and drank all our money away on the first night and we were really depressed. Some old dude had been watching us for hours, and when we were leaving the casino he propositioned us! My friend was really lit and she told him he couldn't afford us, but he asked 'How much?' She was yanking his chain and she said 'How much you got?' He said $500 apiece! He pulled out this big wad of cash and peeled off $2000! I don't know why we did it, but we followed him to his room. At first we just danced for him, but one thing led to another and he got his money's worth. I felt like shit afterwards. Please don't tell anybody, okay?"

Sheila W. 27
laundry service worker

21 the internet

"We've all done it—if you find yourself hunting for old boyfriends on the internet you're just, like, recycling your old trash, and that's proof that your life is in the toilet. Get off the computer and, like, get a real life!"
Celeste H. 38
waitress

"When I left my boyfriend I went online to look for some new friends. It was my first time so I had to create a profile about myself. I put in all kinds of cool shit. Most of it was lies, but it wasn't my fault—it makes you want to lie. They ask you all kinds of questions that make you look stupid if you don't put the right answers in. Who is my favorite author and what books have I read?—I mean, *really*. I did a search for books that smart people read, and I wrote those in. I even put that I'm writing a book about my life. And, am I athletic?—*Fuck, yeah!* I said I ride a bicycle all the time. Well, my ex-boyfriend did—same thing, right? And those little boxes they make you check—they drive me crazy, but it's the easiest lies I ever told. It asked if I'm looking for a permanent relationship, and what the hell am I supposed to say?—'No, I just need a ride home from the bar, and I'll have sex with you for it?'"
Caitlyn W. 23
college student

"My friends don't seem to know that the naked photos they send to strangers will come back to haunt them. My husband is a software engineer and he showed me how easy it is to recover anyone's prior online activity. Nothing ever disappears on the internet. He made a file of all the nude photos one of my friends had sent over the internet, and we emailed it to her—she just about died! She wouldn't believe me before, but she believes me now. It's not just the computer, either—it works for cell phones too. There are websites that people send their candid photos to, just so you can find out what your wife or girlfriend did in the past. They even use names to make the search easier."

Kathee G. 32
marine biologist

"My sister found some guy online and she ended up selling her house and moving four states away for this man she'd never met. She started talking about him like she'd known him for years. I think he hypnotized her, because she didn't seem like herself. My whole family tried to talk her out of it, but she wouldn't listen. She really believed he was Prince Charming. We all crossed our fingers when she left, but we knew something bad would happen. Three months later she called my mom for bus fare to get back home. She left with almost $50,000 and she came back broke. She won't tell me what happened, but I know it was pretty bad."

Loni S. 42
family business

"I got bored so I left my husband behind and flew back home. While I was away I started cruising the dating sites. My daughter was doing it and she seemed to be having fun, so why not? I couldn't believe how many responses I got. I had men driving hundreds of miles just to see me—okay, sleep with me. When I ran out of money my parents kicked me out, so I apologized to my husband and went back home. I told him it was PMS. Of course he quizzed me about what I did while I was gone, and I told him I just sat in my bedroom and cried because I missed him. Just to be safe, I closed my email account and sold my computer to a pawn shop to erase all traces of what I'd done. What I didn't know was, when you close an email account your old email address is available again in ninety days. Three months later my husband opened a new email account with my old address. He went to every dating site there is and clicked on 'forgot password.' He got access to everything I had written to all those men, and everything they wrote to me. One night he asked me casually if I had ever been on a dating site. I flared up and said 'I don't have time for that shit—that's for kids.' He said 'Come here,' as he was pointing at the computer screen. He had seven different windows open on the screen, with all my dating profiles and every message I had sent or received. I mean names, times, dates, locations—you name it!"

Jeannie E. 40
swap-meet vendor

"That's what the internet is for—lying. Sometimes you get money, sometimes you get laid, and sometimes you meet a 60-year-old guy who claimed he was twenty-five. It's a gamble, but what else is there to do?"

Chandra C. 23
unemployed

"I spend more time looking at the women's profiles than I do the men's. A girl needs to know who her competition is. It cracks me up to read the shit women write—*'I like scuba diving, sailing, and mountain climbing'*. What else?—*'traveling, flying, drag racing, motorcycling, bungee jumping'*. No wait, there's more—*'gallery hopping, spelunking, boating, and skiing'*. Give me a break! The women who put this shit in their profiles haven't done it yet, or they went with some guy who was doing it and gave him a blowjob."

Clarissa U. 38
business administrator

"My ex-boyfriend used his cell phone to video us having sex. He set it to video and hid it in the bedroom. When we broke up he put the video on the internet and sent the link to all my friends. There's no way to get it off the internet once it's there."

Madison B. 22
student

"I swear to God, when I'm online I feel like a little girl and I want to pull my dress up. It's not like when I'm with a guy and I can rub my breasts against his arm to tease him. Showing your stuff is the only way to get a reaction online. You just have to be careful because they might be recording you."

Mandi R. 27
ski instructor

"I saw a TV show that made me feel bad for not knowing what my kids were up to on the internet. So I turned on my son's computer when he was at school and I found at least a hundred pictures of his classmates with no clothes on—*Naked!* These are beautiful young girls that he goes to school with, and I know most of them. I almost fainted. If all these girls are doing this online, what are they doing in person? I can't even imagine. I was too embarrassed to approach my son about it, so I made his dad do it."

Keslin Y. 35
middle-school teacher

"Dating sites are addictive. It's too easy to get a guy to want you, and you can make him believe anything you like. Sometimes I'm a whore, and other times I make them believe I'm younger than I really am, and inexperienced. They really love that. I go online when I get home from work, and I can have a guy at my door with candy and flowers and in my bed in less than an hour. It's easier than ordering pizza."

Monica V. 26
Red Cross worker

"I was married for twenty-four years. I started playing pinochle online and I met some really nice people. This one person who called himself Pat was always asking me to go private so he could I.M. me without having anyone else see our conversations. I ignored him at first, but he seemed sincere so I finally gave him my email address. We emailed and talked on the phone for about a year, and he was the most understanding man I'd ever met. I know this sounds stupid, but I fell in love with him and I divorced my husband. When we started making plans to be together, he became reluctant. He said he needed time to make enough money to be able to take care of me. I told him I had money, but he still resisted. His evasiveness made me suspicious so I hired a private investigator in his town to check up on him. I needed to know if there was anything he'd lied about—like a wife. My best guess was that he was married. It only took the private investigator two days to find out everything there was to know about Pat. He sent me photos and everything. Pat was a woman."

Delilah A. 46
special-needs caregiver

how to: translate a woman's online dating profile

"A little more to love" *really means:*
- Dinner won't be cheap.
- I only wear muumuu dresses.
- Can you tell me what color my toenails are?

"I've never been on a dating site before" *really means:*
- I'm on every dating site there is, but with different names.
- I hope you don't find the porn-site photos I posted.
- I only leave my computer to eat and go pee.

"I like snuggling on the couch" *really means:*
- I also have a bed.
- You can do me on the first date if you order the pizza.
- I'd rather have sex than all that other shit I said.

"I love to travel" *really means:*
- You have a car, right?
- Have your credit card ready if you want to get lucky.
- I'm bored, and you *will* take me somewhere.

"I'm divorced" *really means:*
- My ex-husband is still stalking me.
- I live on alimony and child support—*Boom!*
- I still owe my attorney $16,000.

"I have children, but they're not living with me" *really means:*
- Well, they weren't when I wrote this.
- My son gets paroled next month, and where else is he supposed to go?
- The courts took them away from me.

"I drink socially" *really means:*
- Last weekend is nothing but a blur.
- They start mixing my *usual* as soon as I walk in the bar.
- I don't know how I got these rug burns on my forehead.

"I smoke occasionally" *really means:*
- My friends nicknamed me *Virginia Slim*.
- Wanna see my souvenir ashtray collection?
- You could, like, smoke a salmon in my living room.

"I have pets" *really means:*
- My entire life is covered with cat hair.
- I love my dogs more than I could ever love you.
- I'm operating an illegal animal shelter in my spare bedroom.

22 a man's view

◆ about women

"I don't know how she does it. When she's in her mood she can suck the air out of a room. I can barely get enough breath to ask 'What's wrong, baby?' and she'll say 'Nothing.' And then I need an oxygen bottle."
    Kenny W. 38
    heavy-equipment operator

"The way a woman dresses predicts her future. Women who dress like hookers are just lazy—they seem to think two sizes too small is sexy. My girlfriend always looks very classy and she doesn't show too much. She knows something about fashion that a lot of women don't."
    Richard A. 50
    bulk fuel dealer

"Every girl I meet sends me nude photos on my cell phone—that's how they do it. I showed my dad and he couldn't believe it. He said the first naked girl he saw was my mom. I said 'That's weird, Dad—now give my phone back.'"
    Rick U. 24
    sporting-goods sales rep

"My wife is great. What she lacks in love for me, she makes up for in hatred for the women I work with."

Albert G. 39
diesel mechanic

"The thing about being a woman that must be pretty cool is that everybody *always* wants one. Women only want us when they feel like it. I guess we're seasonal."

Sean C. 42
refinery manager

"I got sick and tired of listening to her bitch constantly. I jerked her off the couch and said 'What the hell do you *want?!*' She called me stupid and ran off with her hands over her ears."

Robert K. 41
truck driver

"Seriously, if you stand on a street corner and watch the cars go by and look for who's talking on a cell phone or texting, it's always women. They're dangerous drivers and, just like at home, they can't stop talking. They want to call it multi-tasking—yeah, sure! I'm going to go sit at the bar and call it *lubricated social evaluation.*"

Kerry T. 27
recycling

"Women start acting like they're disgusted after the first date, and it only gets worse. I think they're all just miserable."

Jason M. 41
route driver

"Fat girls hate guys who happen to like fat girls. I like full-figured women myself, but they get out of bed in the morning and accuse me of having bad taste for sleeping with them. This one girl asked me 'Why did you want me?—because all the skinny girls were taken?' I still like them, though."

Jerry S. 29
beverage distributor

"Women call themselves bitches, and then act the part to prove it. And I'm supposed to find this *attractive?* I'm thinking more along the lines of a one-night stand."

Charles D. 36
property manager

"I hate fake boobs. I've had handfuls of both, real and fake, and I like the real ones. Big or small, it doesn't matter. Fake feels fake, no matter how much they spent. I want a girl who's real and natural, not part plastic. What if I stuffed a sock in my pants to get her to follow me home? What's the difference?"

Rodney M. 46
surveyor

"My wife stares at other women and studies them from head to toe, and she doesn't try to hide it. If I even glance at another woman I'm cut off for a week. Equal rights, my ass!"

Mason A. 28
insurance agent

"They call *us* controlling? What the hell else are we supposed to be when they're completely out-of-control? They refuse to take responsibility for anything. They'll demand that we take charge of things, but then they're resentful and childish when we do. Somebody's got to be in control, right?"

John E. 44
estate planning

"I finally learned to stay away from the good-looking women. They have men chasing them all the time, and it fucks up their thinking. I was just another dope in a big long line. Average-looking girls actually have hearts."

Andy J. 33
excavator operator

"My mom taught me to hold the door for a lady, but if I do a lot of them glare at me and go to another door—like I did something wrong."

Michael D. 38
general contractor

"When I was thirteen my grandma told me to stay away from the bushes because bad girls hide in the bushes, and they grab boys and do horrible things to them. I spent years strolling past every bush I could find, and—crickets. I started whistling and walking even slower, but no luck. I finally realized my grandma was pulling my leg. Or maybe that's how she got my grandpa."

Sam P. 31
sports columnist

✧ psycho*therapy*

"My wife was seriously mentally ill for years and nobody would believe me. I got calls at work from our landlord telling me that she was naked out on the roof of our apartment building, and crazy shit like that. I almost lost my job because of it. We went to a shrink and she told me that my wife was fine, and I was the problem. No shit, she blamed it on me! My wife got so violent I had to leave. Finally they diagnosed her and she went to a mental hospital. Needless to say, I don't have much faith in psychologists—especially *women* psychologists."

Terry W. 52
medical technician

"I work in the rehab center at a mental-health clinic, and half the women who work there are making drug connections with the 'recovering' addicts, for themselves or for their deadbeat boyfriends."

James N. 40
rehab counselor

"My wife and I had a really rough time after I came home from work early one day and caught her in bed with my best friend. I begged her to go to marriage counseling, and she went one time. On our second appointment she didn't show up. I sat there for thirty minutes whining about what had happened, and I told the therapist in great detail how this all came about. He said 'You seem to have a good handle on everything that's happened.' I said 'Yes, I do.' He asked 'So, what are you going to do about it?' I repeated what he said—'What am I going to do about it?' My life changed right there on the spot. I finally did something about it, and it was the best $125 I ever spent."

David Y. 53
airline pilot

"I love female therapists. I've done three of them. They always have a really screwed-up past, and they don't have anybody to tell about it, except me. And they fuck like rabbits. I don't go to the bars to find girls—I go to the mental health clinic."

Alan R. 35
self-unemployed

✧ sex

"I play bass guitar every weekend—I get laid every weekend. So do the other band members. It's part of the job."
Ronny I. 36
musician

"You know why they don't set women up on those sexual-predator shows?—because too many men would have to tell on the women who taught them about sex. Young boys like it and they're usually gentlemen about it. My babysitter was giving me blowjobs when I was twelve, and she taught me how to please a woman. It was the most fascinating time of my life. It came in pretty handy in high school. She was the coolest woman I ever knew. Girls are just as horny at twelve, but they can't resist the attention they get from playing the victim."
Harold T. 34
cable guy

"She was horny as hell before we got married. She said she wanted to wait until our honeymoon and I thought that was cool. Then, two months before the wedding she attacked me. It was wild! Now it's like she's grossed-out if I even touch her."
Mark M. 29
auto mechanic

"My wife made me wait until I was fifty to get my Harley. I had other bikes, but she really had a problem with the idea of a Harley. I thought it was just because they cost more. When I finally got my Harley, I had women walking right up to me wanting me to take them for a ride. No shit—women from sixteen to seventy were ready to take off their clothes just for a ride. I thought it was cool at first, but I wondered how many Harleys my wife had been on, and what she had done for the ride. When I asked her, she just grinned."
Calvin S. 56
stonemason

"Go to church—get laid! Church is the best place to find horny women, praise the lord."
Glenn P. 46
software company executive

"When I tell my friends how many women answer the door naked, they don't believe me. It happens all the time, and it puts me way behind schedule."
Greg W. 32
parcel delivery driver

"Sex is the cure for everything. My wife has chronic headaches, but after four orgasms her headache is gone. It's a miracle! When she's mad at me—four orgasms, and she can't remember why she was mad."
Curtis G. 38
city architect

"I rented a room from a woman when I was in college. When her car broke down and I fixed it, she apologized because she couldn't pay me for it. So she offered me a blowjob instead. She said I wasn't the only one with tools of the trade."
Devin E. 31
certified public accountant

"When we walk into a bar we look for the best-dressed woman in the place. What women don't understand is, when they take off the fancy clothes, hose off all the makeup and kick off the stilettos, they all look alike. But they don't want you to see them like that. That's why they leave early in the morning."
Will V. 28
college groundskeeper

"I used to enjoy going home and 'sexually assaulting' my wife. Now I'm afraid to go home because my wife and children don't even like me. I'm afraid if I exercise too much authority they might have me thrown in jail for being abusive."
Kenneth S. 42
auto-service manager

"If my wife knew how many times I've been propositioned by women, she'd cut off my balls and I'd be working at a flower shop. A uniform is a green light for women willing to trade sex for leniency."
Anton C. 46
police officer

"You know what scares me?—the size of women's upper arms. *Fuck a duck!* They're getting bigger than my thighs. If I take one home I make sure I'm really nice to her. Can you imagine if she got me in a headlock?"

Stan B. 24
fuel truck driver

"Women like to call me a *'chubby-chaser'*. At first I thought they were making fun of me, but they're really making fun of themselves. I can't help it—I like big girls. There are two problems: It's a struggle to have sex with a big woman—but I like it—and they don't understand why I think they're beautiful. I've been with a lot of big girls, but they don't let me stick around because they're insulted that I'd want to be with them. One girl told me that she was going to lose weight and I wouldn't like her when she's skinny."

Casey D. 26
appliance repair

"There must be some small gang of men with a mission to de-virginize all the women on Earth. I've heard tell that every woman was once a virgin, but *I've* never found one. Who are these men, and where do I sign up?"

Billy M. 35
plumber

"Young girls are okay to fuck, but then they want me to take them shopping. Their parents need to get them their own credit card."

Jack P. 31
payday loans

"I know I'm not supposed to care about her past, but when I found out that half my friends had already fucked her, it was like chewing gum I found stuck under the table."

Joel D. 30
demolition tech

"I can fuck just about any girl I want if I have a few bucks in my pocket, a car and a clean shirt. That's a sad commentary."

Ben S. 27
computer repair

✧ fuck-buddies

"I'm the guy she calls after you drop her off and kiss her on the cheek. I just treat her like a whore and I don't ask her for commitment. Do that, and anybody can be a fuck-buddy."
Trevor H. 39
auto transport

"When I was driving a truck my wife used to make me call her when I was an hour from home to make sure I was safe, and so she didn't worry. I thought 'Damn, this woman loves me.' She was screwing my neighbor Dave. And he still has my lawnmower!"
Brent K. 42
electrician

✧ penis size

"I was working out-of-town for two months and my ex-wife wanted to know where I'd been—like it was any of her business. I felt like fucking with her so I told her I'd had surgery. She asked 'For what?' I said that I'd had my penis enlarged so I could keep up with all her fuck-buddies. She wanted to see me immediately! Is that what I was married to?"
Roger G. 47
communications equipment installer

"Penis size isn't a problem—penis *count* is. I only have one, but my girlfriend wasn't happy with just one. I thought I was competing with quality until I found out it was quantity she was after! I used to feel bad about my size, but now I feel bad about how many penises I have. How the hell am I supposed to compete with that?"
Ivan T. 26
radio personality

"My wife divorced me and she hooked up again with her party friends. In two days my phone started ringing—it was her friends calling. They said she had bragged about me being well-hung, and they were worried that I might be lonely."
Kyle F. 41
petroleum engineer

"In the army I showered with white guys who made some of the black guys wrap an extra towel around them to hide their shortcomings. But the black guys still get all the publicity."
Victor H. 36
security dog trainer

"When my wife hit 275 pounds it was really hard to make love to her. Right in the middle of sex she'd yell 'Deeper, deeper!' I wondered if my pecker had shrunk since our honeymoon. I finally figured out that her thighs were so big I couldn't even reach her vagina. I shouldn't have told her because when I did she went to live with her parents. Now she's easy 350."
Terry W. 37
oilfield service

"I got tired of girls telling me they'd had bigger. They're obsessed with size. When the last girl I dated told me that, I said 'No, you didn't—the guy you were fucking did. If *you* had bigger, whip it out and amaze me.' At least she shut up about it after that."
Patrick A. 23
college student

"Women talk about penis size like they have one. Why don't they talk about vagina size? I'm hung like a porn star, but these women's bodies are so atrophied from laziness and having kids, it's like throwing a hotdog down a hallway."
Seth B. 30
bus driver

◇ lies

"When I was growing up my sister and I were used to waking up to a different man sitting at the kitchen table every morning. They were always having coffee and wearing my mom's robe. When I brought my fiancée to meet my family, my mom told her that she herself had only been with three men in her whole life. I busted out laughing, and my mom chased me around with the lawn sprinkler trying to kill me."
Jason N. 29
painter

"I caught my wife lying to me, and I proved it. She said 'You're not supposed to call me a liar.' I said 'But I caught you in three different lies!' She said 'Yeah, but you're not supposed to call me a liar to my face—that's rude!'"

Sonny R. 46
building maintenance

"A few years after we got married, my wife started putting on weight and ballooned up to about 375 pounds. She said it was her thyroid, but she wouldn't go to the doctor. I caught her hiding food on my mother's back porch—stuff like doughnuts and candy. Then I searched our house and found her stash. It was like she was hiding drugs or something! She was sitting on the bed, and I pulled up a chair and held her hand to talk with her about it. She fell back on the bed, and then rolled off on the floor and started hitting it with her fists, and kicking her feet and yelling *'I want my mommy!'* I swear to God I'm not lying."

Thom Q. 41
airfield service crew

jealousy

"Jewelry boxes and photo albums are designed to make men jealous. They show you their jewelry one piece at a time, and tell you the story about where they got it and who gave it to them. Then they pick up something and put it down quickly without explaining, so you feel obligated to ask 'And that one..?' Then they put on their 'reluctant' act and say 'Well, if you must know...' And then you hear the story about the NFL player they met in a bar, and he flew her to Paris and bought her this little necklace. And then she says 'Don't worry, we're just friends.'"

Jesse L. 32
landscaping

"I played guitar for my daughter ever since she was born. At five years old she had perfect pitch and she could sing harmony like an angel. All our friends told us we should make a recording and send it to somebody who could do something with it. My wife got so jealous she kicked a hole through the front of my guitar, and refused to let me sing with my daughter anymore. We divorced

shortly after that and I didn't sing with my daughter again until she was eighteen, but her mother put a stop to that—again. The memory of her beautiful voice still gives me chills."
Michael S. 37
forklift sales

"My wife taught me how jealousy is a disease. And it's incurable. I worked with a lot of women and she couldn't stand it. Every single day she'd accuse me of wanting to be with another woman, and I spent every evening trying to convince her that I loved her, and only her. It didn't work. Someone told me that I should get my wife's name tattooed on my chest and that would cure the jealousy. My wife and I got matching tattoos with each other's names, and guess what?—that didn't work either. We've been apart for years, but we talk now and then and she told me the only effect that tattoo had was to make her new boyfriends jealous."
Arthur T. 43
human resources

✧ relationships & marriage

"I was a perfect gentleman when I dated a beautiful girl from a good family. Her parents insisted on meeting me before they let her get in my car. I thought I'd found my soulmate—a girl with some background and morals. It felt good because I'm not a back-seat-of-the-car kind of guy. We hugged after our first date, and I promised to call the next day. On our second date we were watching the sunset at the beach and she pulled away from me, crossed her arms, and asked 'Are we *ever* going to fuck?'"
Daniel K. 29
medical student

"If you aren't ready to have sex on the first date with these women, they'll say 'You're gay, aren't you?'"
Larry N. 41
grocery store manager

"Women don't like who you are—they like what you have, what you do, or what you can buy for them."
Jacob Q. 32
financial services executive

"I'm older and wiser and I've learned an important lesson about matters of the heart. When it comes to women, make sure they have one—because not all of them do."
    Howard G. 64
    lumber broker

"The trouble with marrying a whore is that you're the only one who doesn't know that's what she is."
    Christopher W. 24
    machine operator

"I just went to the store and got propositioned by a 25-year-old girl, and I'm fifty-six! Jesus Christ, my daughter is older than her! What's going on here?"
    Red R. 56
    car dealer

"What does it it mean when women like bad boys? Even my sister told me that I treat women too good, and that's why they leave. It's confusing."
    Greer T. 47
    concrete contractor

"Why do women insist that the past is the past, and then quiz me about mine?"
    Bret A. 28
    dialysis technician

"I was riding my motorcycle across the country to ask my girlfriend to marry me. I got a motel room in Kansas that had a huge sports bar. I went for a drink before bed, and it was just me and the bartender in there. She was tiny and pretty, and we talked for a couple of hours about my trip. She'd seen me pull up on the motorcycle and she said 'Listen, this thing with your girlfriend isn't going to work out, so let's get on your motorcycle and you can take me to Arizona instead.' I said I was flattered but I loved my girlfriend, and the next day I rode off. When I got back east we were married, and it lasted two months because her mother didn't approve. My little bartender was right. I still have the picture I took of her, and sometimes I look at it and wonder if she still works there."
    Thomas Y. 50
    manufacturing consultant

"When I turned forty I got to where I couldn't get a stiffy anymore, and my wife seemed pleased about it. I went to the doctor and he asked me how things were at home. I told him a little about things between us, and he said 'Don't worry, it's not you.' I finally got tired of her bitchy attitude and we separated. Then I met a woman who wasn't miserable about everything, and my problem went away. It was like I was eighteen again! Living with a bitch will take the lead out of your pencil."

Bryan T. 47
marketing executive

"What's wrong with wanting to marry a virgin? Women get so pissed-off if they even hear the word, like it's something gross. I'm a virgin and I think I deserve to marry someone like me."

Gary K. 26
family business

"Women are always saying that men won't commit—but commit to what, exactly? It's *bullshit!* I've been ready for years for a woman I could love completely, but I can't find one who's worth it. They're the ones who are incapable of commitment. A woman's life is one big lie—just an excuse for driving men away with their infantile anger and bitterness. And then the *blame..!* Women have thrown away the magic they used to own because someone told them they needed a set of balls."

Peter L. 46
loan officer

"If she's divorced with a couple of kids, she's so engrossed in her family that you don't have a chance of ever being important to her. But she'll swear that you are."

Trenton D. 43
fairgrounds director

"There's no way I can convince my son that there are good girls out there. He just looks at me like I've lost my mind. He has girls driving to his apartment every night to sleep with him—sometimes two at a time!"

Dean L. 48
electrician

"My wife is my best friend, and you know why?—because she doesn't just talk, she listens. All women talk, but that doesn't make a relationship."

Frank E. 47
school principal

"A woman used to look forward to depending on a man. Now they live in fear of something happening to him, or of being abandoned for a younger woman. They don't know how to take care of themselves. My mother never worked, and when my dad died Mom was set for life because he left a life-insurance policy to take care of us. I guess that's too old-fashioned."

Kevin R. 49
investment advisor

"Here's the paradox: The most beautiful and most educated women I know of are with the most pitiful examples of manhood. Do these bad-boy alcoholics and drug users who abuse women know something I don't?"

Sid L. 37
attorney

◆ children & parenting

"My wife decided to use drugs and go to jail, so I raised my daughter by myself for years. I can tell you this: A girl will behave like her mother regardless of what a father teaches her. It's a no-win situation. I want those years back."

Kirk S. 46
furniture manufacturing

"In four years I dated two different women in their fifties. They were both very beautiful and bright. I asked one of them to marry me, but her 36-year-old son wouldn't allow it. He was still living at home and felt threatened by my proposal, so he got mad and punched a hole in the wall. She told me that he had been through a lot when he was a child. The other woman had *two* adult sons living at home, and one of them stole her car and totaled it. When I saw her walking in the rain to work, completely drenched, I really thought she'd realize that she was the reason her boys never grew

up. But, nope—they're all still together. What a waste of two fine women."
James D. 52
internal affairs officer

✧ mothers

"My grandma always told me 'Do unto others as you would have them do unto you, but not necessarily when it comes to women. Watch out for those women."
Danny A. 59
geologist

"My wife said 'I want to trust you, but my family has more checkbooks than you. There's security in numbers, and they'll give me money no matter what I do."
Colin J. 34
aerospace engineer

"I've never made love to a real woman in America—I've only made love to some mother's daughter."
Hans V. 37
automotive design engineer

"Spoiled women don't ever see it coming. Their looks fade, they get mean and fat, and then one day nobody wants to take care of them. Then all that's left is Mommy and Daddy's money."
Randy E. 54
highway contractor

✧ the internet

"I met a woman online who said she was a proper lady and didn't go to bars, and she didn't want to meet anyone who did. That was me! We met for coffee, exchanged last names, and I told her I wanted to see her again. When I got home my daughter searched the internet and found pictures of her in some club, and a male stripper was giving her a lap dance. Thank you, internet!"
Robert I. 44
personal trainer

✧ fighting dirty

"Just dating a woman increases your chances of ending up in jail."
  Theo V. 31
  bartender

"I found out my wife spent the day with some guy she worked with, and we started arguing. She butted me in the forehead and broke her nose—I couldn't believe it. I took her to the doctor and he said she'd be fine, but it blacked both her eyes and she got a lot of mileage out of that. Her sisters assumed that I had beaten her. She told them it was an accident, but she let them believe that she was really covering for me. They all hated me and I spent the next month defending myself. We never finished the argument over her co-worker—she's not stupid."
  Alex G. 42
  tire sales

"My wife can watch a TV show about some guy having an affair, and I get treated like a cheating scumbag husband for the next week. Don't tell *me* television doesn't influence our thinking."
  Otto M. 24
  industrial supplies distributor

"My ex-wife advised me that the key to happiness is to find an ugly girl. She said it was the secret to a man's happiness, and she cared so much for me that she couldn't hold out on me any longer. She also confided that she didn't want me anymore, but she didn't want anyone else to have me either. I wonder what her new husband would think about our conversation."
  Evan L. 42
  stockbroker

"My mother-in-law calls my wife a 'weed-eater' of men. She knows her daughter well."
  Tim N. 36
  musician

"When my elderly mother became ill she hired an attorney to draw up a will. My sister always believed that she would be the executor because she was the oldest. My mother appointed me instead, and my sister was livid. So my sister called the neighbors and told them I was having sex with my mother. The neighbors would glare and

gesture at me from across the street. The best part about it was that the will revealed my mother had already spent all her money. I was delighted. The easiest will to execute is one with no wealth to bequeath. My mother passed owing $5,000 to the IRS, and my sister and I inherited nothing. Touché, Sis!"
 Mike G. 51
 crane operator

"I was waiting for a business associate in the lounge, and seven women came in to get tuned-up for their *girl's night out*. They were only two tables away and I could hear everything they said. I heard them refer to their husbands and boyfriends as 'assholes' at least twenty times in as many minutes. I didn't offer to buy them a drink."
 Stephen K. 45
 medical doctor

"What makes a woman wait a year to talk about her past? And who gives a shit anyway? She had sex with me on our first date—am I supposed to think I was the first one she did it with? Why not just shut up about it? She likes to bring it up when she argues with me, and she says I don't love her because I don't care how many guys she fucked. She makes me tired."
 Mark P. 27
 border patrol agent

"My wife is always mad at me and she says I'll never understand what it's like to be a woman. Okay, soooo, does that make me sub-human? I don't *want* to know what it's like to be a woman. I'm still learning what it's like to be a man. Why didn't she tell me about her prejudice toward men before we were married and she was still giving me blowjobs?"
 Lance B. 26
 ranch hand

"I wouldn't let my wife buy new furniture because we couldn't afford it. All I heard after that was 'Get your hands off me.' I got a part-time job on the side so she could buy her furniture, but she's still mad and I still can't put my hands on her. I should have bought a motorcycle instead."
 Bruce K. 33
 backhoe operator

"No shit, this really happened. I was working two jobs, and I was running late for work. I asked my wife if she would roll the trash out to the curb because I really needed it empty for the weekend. She said 'Sure.' When I got home the trash can was still next to the house, and still full of trash. I swear, all I said was 'Honey, the trash...' and she went off on me and yelled 'Why don't *you* ever take the trash out?!' I reminded her that I always do, but she just got angrier. It's like living with a mental patient—she makes no sense at all."

Donald K. 32
gardener/laborer

"Women suffer from self-induced discontent, and they want nothing more than to inflict it on men."

Scott H. 46
attorney

✧ women, bars & nightclubs

"Women try to get a man to talk about himself first because they all think they're psychologists. Well, until their third drink, and then you can't shut them up—where they've been, who they've been with—and then they start name-dropping. If you want to take them home though, you have to pretend to listen and be interested."

Greg R. 52
cabinetmaker/finish carpenter

"Whatever happened to women like Carrie Nation? The only time she walked into a bar was to hack it to pieces. That kind of woman turns me on. If a woman really wanted something back then, she had her way with it. Have you looked at women lately? They used to be our most valuable asset, and now they dress like prostitutes and trade sex for free drinks. I miss Carrie."

Walter W. 64
wealth management advisor

23 married & loving it

"I was spoiled rotten when I got married because I grew up getting everything I wanted. So who do I marry?—a man who says we can't afford it all. I wanted a divorce after the first month. I had no idea how much he loved me until I was eight months pregnant and my daughter was delivered still-born. I really needed someone to suffer with so I turned to my mother, but she just didn't get it. I was too hard-headed to see that my husband was also in pain, or that he had anything of value to say to me. Now he's my best friend and even though we have a painful history, it made us closer. I'd made it my own personal tragedy, but when I gave up thinking it happened only to me it became *our* grief to carry, and our healing to share. Someone should have slapped the shit out of me a long time ago. I know now that we'll die in each other's arms."
Misty E. 39
marketing guru

"I love my husband and I'd rather be with him than anyone. My co-workers hate me for it. Two of them wanted to get him alone to show me how wrong I am about him. I told them to go fuck off! Thank God my husband is my best friend because nobody I work with is a friend."
Mary F. 46
internet advertising

"A woman will never know how fantastic making love can be until she's struggled through twenty-five years with a man she chose because she held out for the best one. You work your bloody ass off and put your heart and soul into raising two children, get them through college, and teach them to make it on their own. Going to bed with the man who suffered through this with you is a powerful aphrodisiac, and no pill or battery-operated device can even come close. If he's a good man his only goal is to give us what we want—children, a home, and security. Men want children because we want children. They're just providing for our instincts. If a man only cared about his own instincts he'd be living on a boat or on some deserted island. What women fail at is getting the man off his boat and onto *our* island. It starts with respect and intimacy. It's an investment in the future that grows in value over a long time. Too many women demand the payoff up front, and that's foolish and immature. Learning to make love together and raise our children together was just foreplay. Our foreplay has lasted for twenty-five years and we've just begun to know what intimacy truly feels like."

Karol V. 51
high-school principal

"Women hate men who want a virgin, because they lost theirs at a party in junior high. I graduated from high school and worked for two years before I considered giving mine away. But that's the reason weddings are getting so expensive—because they're trying to replace their virginity with a huge celebration. They'll wear a fancy white gown that costs as much as a new car, when they've been sleeping with the groom for two years and half the wedding party before that! It's like going to a funeral with an empty casket."

Kassandra T. 34
college admissions

"To decide that all men are alike is the stupidest thing a woman can do, but most of them have. Do they really think that the losers they've slept with prove anything about men? I took my time finding a really good man, and I'm glad I did. There are bad people all over the place, but if you have half a brain you look for a good one. A woman should take her time to pick the father of her children."

Remy V. 27
home business

"My brother was a hell-raiser before he got married, but after his wedding his friends said he just dropped out of sight. They called me and even came to my house because he wouldn't party or go hunting with them anymore. They thought he was pussy-whipped. His wife flew home to Thailand to see her family for a week, and I finally got him alone to find out why the hell he had dumped his friends. He made me promise not to tell anybody, but every day when he comes home from work his wife takes off his clothes, hands him a beer, gives him a blowjob and then serves him dinner. I wondered what my husband would do if I started doing that. The first time I met him at the door and started undressing him, he asked me if I had wrecked the car or bounced a check, but now he *never* works late."

Charlie D. 27
housewife/sex goddess

"My ex-husband married the ugliest woman I've ever seen. I felt pretty gorgeous when I first saw her, but they've been together for eleven years now and all our old friends love her to death. They say she's the nicest person and she treats him like a king. I try to get him in bed when he comes over to pick up the kids, and he acts like I have the plague. Even my kids love her!"

Debra A. 46
proofreader

"Marriage is a contract with God, your husband, and everyone who came to your wedding. Your guests even pay you in advance for keeping your promise, by giving you gifts. Good luck finding a job that pays you in advance for your promise to show up for work. If women treated their business obligations like they do their marriages, they'd all be in jail for breach-of-contract! These women don't give a damn about breaking their promises, and our laws turn a blind eye. I think judges believe a woman isn't capable of living up to a contract so they give them the house, the kids, and half his paycheck to shut them up. And then they go and collect welfare! My husband keeps his promises, and I keep mine. We built our entire life on our promises, and we love each other because we meant what we said at our wedding. We didn't get married for the gifts or the attention, and we never had an escape plan."

Martha Q. 57
county clerk/recorder

"A decent relationship has little to do with feelings—it's got to do with how dedicated you are and how you treat each other. Dedication happens first, and the good feelings come from that because of your love and respect for each other. I trust my husband to drive our promiscuous, oversexed babysitter home on Friday night. He always refuses though, so I have to get the kids out of bed and we drive her home together. I love that man."

Faye W. 28
retail sales

"It's like this: I don't feel like having sex as much as he does, but I do it. He doesn't feel like getting up at three o'clock in the morning to change the baby, but he does. Sometimes I don't want to be a mother of three kids, so he does it. I've got his back, and he's got mine—that's marriage."

Judith Q. 36
home daycare business

"Why don't women know that there's nothing more productive than a relationship with a good man? I mean financially, emotionally, and for every other reason. It might sound mechanical, but survival is what drives us to be together in the first place, and why not? It's better than having your parents support you until they die. My marriage is everything to me. If other women want to laugh at me for being happy—*Screw them!*"

Sue J. 48
delivery driver

"Mexican women are taught to never deny their husbands sex, even if we're mad at them. American women take away sex to punish a man, and look what happens—divorce."

Maria C. 49
store manager

"I worked with my husband for fifteen years. We owned a little restaurant—he cooked and I waited tables. We loved being together 24/7. You wouldn't believe how many women chewed me out for spending too much time with him. They said they couldn't stand to be with their husbands half that much. They needed their *'me time'*. I *loved* to work with my husband, but I was always in trouble for it. It's not as if I could slap their teeth out for insulting my life—they were our customers. When we lost the lease on our building we had to close the restaurant and find regular jobs. We thought we were going to die. We spend all day missing each other, and I'm miserable without him."

Lorna O. 45
bank teller

"My husband is a remarkable lover, and I can't wait to get home after work. He helps me with dinner and the dishes. We put the kids to bed together, and my cheeks flush when he touches my neck. My friends accuse me of being controlled and mentally abused. If what he does to me is all that, I want more! They're just mad because I won't go out to the bars with them. They wouldn't go either if they were married to my husband."

Toni B. 37
self-employed

"I run my husband's bath for him, and I bathe him too. He buys my food and clothes and he gives me a nice place to live. He loves me, and I love him. That's not popular, is it?"

Oyuki Z. 30
language teacher

"We got married way too young, but somehow we've stayed together for seventeen years. The only thing we had in common was that we were both party freaks and we did drugs. One day we woke up clean and sober, working adults with a mortgage. We were bored to death. We decided to get a divorce because there was just nothing there anymore. My husband felt sad about it, and he thought maybe we should go to counseling before we filed the papers. I said okay. We told the counselor our story and he agreed that our relationship was probably over, but he asked us to do him a favor. He wanted us to spend the next week complimenting one another and talking about all the things we had loved about each other. It sounded stupid, but we agreed. We kept our promise, and we traded compliments back and forth until we got nauseated. On about the third day my husband told me how beautiful he thought I was, and I started crying. I couldn't stop, and then he started crying too. We held each other for over an hour, and we did something we'd never done before—we fell in love."

Junie W. 35
jewelry designer

aftershock

poet ['pōet; 'pōit] noun

1. a person who writes poems.
2. a person possessing special powers of imagination or expression.

From a man's point of view, women possess an immense and mysterious natural creative power. We may not understand it, but we can't resist it, and none of us doubts that it can either break us or inspire us. We love you, we want you, and we always have. If we are honest with ourselves, our truest desire is to be able to trust your God-given power, because it inspires in us a gentle kind of greatness we seem unable to find in ourselves. If you could see in yourselves what we see in you, just imagine what we could do together. If you dare to dream a more beautiful world, we'll sell our souls to build it for you.

A friend of mine wrote some letters to a woman he loves, and when he shared them with me I was moved unexpectedly to tears. This guy doesn't look like a romantic poet, though I can't say I know how one should look. He's worn around the edges, and lately a little on the downside of advantage. You'd barely notice him if you passed him at the grocery store or on the street, but something unpredictable burns inside of him. Here's the thing—there's a roughneck *and* a poet in all of us. I think we'll find both if we look with our hearts instead of our eyes. We may also find a little raw naked truth of our own. Poets sometimes have a habit of illuminating places we've darkened, intentionally or not, imploring us to wake up. I can't think of a better conclusion to the book than to share two of my friend's letters as a reminder that you probably really shouldn't judge a thing by its cover.

Alec

MY FRIEND EMILY

JULY 25, 2009

My dear friend, how can I tell you what you have done for me? I want to thank you for your kindness and your friendship. Your beautiful smile and your charming spirit have endeared you to me. Your creative ambition and fearless confidence inspire me. I like the way you live your life and fiercely love your friends. I trust the sincerity in your eyes, as I try to name that lovely, soft, changeable color. I feel good when I am near you. I like the shape of your feet. I giggle like a kid when I know I'll be seeing you soon. You have become completely indispensable to me. The world just seems right, knowing you are in it. Some days ago my strange imagination carried me off to a future day when I'll hear the news that you are leaving, and it broke my heart. I'm astonished at how deeply I've come to care for you. What is also impossible for me to ignore is that I am being changed from inside, and it's because of you.

A bright new thing is being made of the dust that had settled in my neglected corners. Blown aloft in the gentlest and most unassuming way, it sparkles in light of an unfamiliar color, and I am drunk on it. It refuses to collect again in the patterns I knew, and I don't want it to. This is some sublime state of uncertain possibility.

Do I make too much of this? What happened? Two friends' lives just brushed past each other a little more closely than before, and something rubbed off and got inside me. My heart is learning from yours, and I am different. I'm feeling things more intensely than I have in years.

Do you want to know how incredibly valuable you are to me? You are one of a tiny number of spirits who have somehow been able to open me to the bone. All my cells seem to have awakened suddenly. Everything around me is fluttering loose, and life has all my attention. I don't know how it happened—I love my life again. There is more joy in every part of it, old and new. How is it possible to comprehend the value of such a gift?

I am here to freely offer whatever makes your life better—kindness, respect, understanding, knowledge, encouragement, love. I am grateful to know you, and thrilled if I can share something helpful to you. I love our friendship. I love your life with your husband and your friends, love your strength and independence, your biggest dreams and wickedest thoughts, your past and your future. I love you through and through. I'm fucking crazy about you, sister, and I'll be your friend forever, if you want.

So be it—that's what is in me.

Will

Dear Emily

CHAPTER ONE

SUMMER 2010

I awoke at a quarter past midnight on Saturday, July 18, 2009 at the corner of 13th & D Street. I had been asleep, as near as I can tell, for about sixteen years. There in the middle of the street on your two wheels, under a brilliant backdrop of summer stars, you broke me open.

Strange that it happened in a place called Salida, because I walked right out of my old life that night, and began a new one. You didn't know it, and didn't intend it, but something came over me then and I haven't been the same since.

We rode through the quiet darkness on smooth, empty streets that still radiated warmth from the day. We rode past little houses and under enormous rustling cottonwoods. I loved being alone with you. I would not have traded places with anyone on Earth that night. The picture of you sitting upright in your little gray dress and sandals, weaving across the wide pavement, enchants me still. You seemed to float without a care in the world as we neared our destination. You reached the corner and made the left turn ahead of me. Your feet left the pedals and you kicked your bare legs playfully out to the sides and coasted into the rear driveway of the old motel. A giant, soft wave of joy crashed down and enveloped me and a warm swell rose inside me and flushed my face. My heart had been stolen by the spirit of a child.

When you stood a few moments later at my door, in your bikini, I nearly came apart. The hot tub was closed for the evening, and so I walked you back across the pavement to your door. I allowed myself a quick glance downward. You went inside and turned to look at me. Time stopped. Solid matter began to blur and dissolve into the dark outer edges of some kind of vortex, until all that existed anywhere was you and me and the thirty inches between us. I heard myself say goodnight to you, and I walked very slowly back to my room. It was a long, long walk and I couldn't seem to get my mouth to close. I laid awake thinking for a long time, and what I thought was that I had just lived one of the best days of my life.

I know it sounds like nothing, but I swear the ground moved that night. My world felt different, but I didn't know just how yet. I was already very fond of you. I truthfully cannot remember ever having such a light and happy heart as when I am near you and I can see your smile. It makes me grateful to be alive to see it. Being with you that night opened my heart and it opened a door for me. I finally had a new perspective. I looked ahead to the end of the road I had been on for many years, and I didn't like what I saw there. I had thought too little of myself for far too long, and made too many apologetic choices out of guilt and resignation. I saw nothing but predictable, uninspiring years of pretense ahead, every trace of trust and intimacy long gone, and a miserable end waiting. I wanted to just let go and let it fall apart.

I turned and started down a new path, and I'm still following it. I have no idea where I'm going, but I feel alive and adventurous again, and I like it. You have made me want something better, and have given me the courage to change. Every day when I wake up, I feel like a different person. I hardly know my mind anymore. Old things are losing their hold and falling away from me, and new ideas are taking root in my head. I have lost my taste for most things in the material world, and have become re-immersed in nature and spirit. I used to be such fun. I could see in you some of the best parts of myself that I had left behind somewhere, especially your love for life, your independence, and your crazy self-confidence. You made me remember what life is supposed to feel like—that it's too important to settle for just ordinary. I think you should know the profound effect you can have on people. You have changed me deeply, and I'll never be the same. There is so much more love in me because of knowing you, I don't know what to do with it all—so much more joy and longing for excitement and adventure. It's as if my life is just now beginning, and I'm going to need to live a long time to finish this exploration. It's no exaggeration to tell you that knowing you has saved my life. How on Earth could I not love you?

  You do not owe me anything, ever. I don't love you because of what you can do for me, I love you for what you have already done for me. If my words don't feel like a gift to you, please forgive me for not saying it right. I know that my alternate reality doesn't seem to fit in this world. I know that I am out of my mind. Mad about you, or just plain mad, I wouldn't blame you for running away from me, fast and far. I know that I can be strange and serious, secretive, reclusive, obsessive—I know it. I've been withdrawn from the social world, and I have some outrageous ideas in my head about reality that almost no one can really take seriously. For some obvious reasons and a few less apparent ones, I don't dare to imagine that I could seem attractive to you. If there's a man in your dreams, I'm pretty sure he doesn't look much like me. I know that you don't feel the way I do, and I still cannot stop thinking about you. You haunt my mind relentlessly, and absolutely everything makes me think of you.

In Paris last fall, I saw you everywhere. The place is filled with overwhelming feminine beauty and intimate little scenes at every turn. It left its impression, but my fondest and most vivid memory is of lying awake at night, every night, thinking of you and watching very white clouds race across the city sky in front of a huge, bright moon. God, how I wanted to be there with you.

Is this nothing but an unhealthy obsession? Whatever it is or isn't, I can't see it as a bad thing. Far from being unhealthy, it has made me care about myself more than ever—physically, spiritually, emotionally. I have grown so much in the last year and have become very aware of what is no longer important to me. What actually is important now is another thing entirely. I am, to say the least, distracted from focusing clearly on my own independent life. I don't know how to go forward until I can get you out of my mind a little, or else somehow deeper in it. I am craving truth and freedom, and a little chaos.

Have I lost my friend? These feelings are my own, and no one can take them from me, not even you. I will love you no matter what you do, and I love you enough to leave you alone if it's what you want. If you have to break my heart, then do it—I'm already broken. Be as kind as you can, but smash it good or I'll never get over you. I know this about myself. Be a warrior—sharpen your biggest sword and cut me to ribbons. Cut me out of your life if you have to. Burn this letter, delete me from your memory and your iPhone. I won't like it, but I'll live. And I'll live better for having known you.

CHAPTER TWO

There's something I kind of like about being a ridiculous, romantic fool. I thought of you as a fresh breeze in my life, come to make everything new and lovely. Then the wind started picking up and blowing parts of me from here to there. I saw too late that I had lost my bearings. You had become a powerful storm that scoured everything in sight. Nothing I know has been left unscathed by your presence in my life. If I wanted to, I could never undo your influence on me. I just have to get at what is under the surface of life. You have made me a restless soul, and I thank God for that.

As plain and true as I know how to say it, this is what is meaningful to me: I love your bright, beautiful mind and your innately wise soul. I love the freedom of your lovely, happy and wild spirit. It jumps out of you in your sparkling laugh, hides in your handwriting and in the clothes you wear, and twirls in your smiling eyes, and it makes me feel like a kid again—like I can do anything.

I love that you call me William. It's kind of you, and I am honored by it. It makes me trust myself. I love the way my name sounds when you say it, and I love how my ear can find your voice in a sea of sounds and pull it close to me.

I love your indomitable nature—that you love yourself enough to change your life and make it what you want it to be. I love that you won't be deterred from a dream by something like fear of the unknown. I love that you don't really need anyone to give you confidence. Do you know how desirable that makes you?

I love that you can be grace incarnate in your perfect navy linen dress one minute, and laughing your silly head off the next.

How do I even begin to tell you how beautiful I think you are? Yum with three m's? Words fail, but what else do I have? I still love your quirky feet. I love your red-delicious hair, the luxurious texture of your skin, and the hypnotic qualities of your miraculous shape. I still have to fight not to look too long at you. I don't know how it's possible, but you seem to be growing more beautiful and confident all the time. You're poised and elegant, and your patient, regal gait is noticeable from a hundred yards away. When in a relaxed mood, you drape exquisitely over, and greatly improve, any lucky chair upon which you may flop. I've lived enough to recognize a fantastic thing when I see one, and I know very well how rare and lovely you are.

But I also see that what makes you beautiful on the outside comes from what is beautiful inside you, and it's the part of you that will last forever. I love dearly what I see in those gorgeous eyes that are so unafraid. That joyful, childlike spirit of yours is only part of the story. There is a powerful, fiery goddess in there looking out at the world, looking through, searching for truth in all other eyes she sees. And I love that you seem to know it. She is your wise, knowing intelligence. She has the biggest heart I've ever known, and she is who you really are, walking around in your body. And she is who will not let go of my soul.

I told you before about looking into your eyes—how it made me want to either crumble or fly. And I know it made you uneasy, but I meant what I said. It's like you see right through to the heart of me. I can't bear to hold a dishonest thought with those eyes looking at me, but I rather like being put on the spot by you. Actually, I believe that I meant every word I ever spoke to you, and I'm glad about that.

One thing, though—I told you that I didn't want anything from you, and you said I should ask myself if that was the truth. I wanted to be a true friend to you—didn't want to ever be needy with you. But I've been asking, and of course you were right. I wanted it all. Every last bit of you. Every corner of your mind, every nook of your body, every dream in your soul. All your dark, scary thoughts and every ecstatic thrill. I wanted to be still and silent with you, and to laugh and cry and sing and scream with you. I wanted to be bored to tears with you, and to bend your imagination all out of shape. I wanted to taste you and smell you and know you inside and out. I wanted to dress you and undress you, wanted to be naked in the sun with you, and buried under piles of blankets with you. I wanted to accept you as a gift, freely offered, and I wanted to just take you. I wanted to forget I ever knew you, and I wanted to never be able to get you out of my heart. I wanted to be wide awake with you, and to go to sleep forever. I wanted to hang on every precious word from your beautiful mouth, and to tell you to shut the hell up and pay attention to your life. I wanted to hold you sweetly and tenderly, and I wanted to stretch you and bend you and tie you in knots. I wanted to be comforting and familiar to you, and I wanted to seem exotic and maybe just a little freaky. I wanted to use you up and burn you out, and to live forever with you, be drunk with you and clear with you and painfully dead-honest with you. I wanted to be strong and invincible in your eyes, and I wanted you to bring me to my knees. I wanted to build you a little house and a studio, and raise a beautiful, loving little red-haired daughter named Edith with you. I wanted to travel the world with you, and to just stay home, to know what it is to miss you desperately, and to never let you out of my sight. I wanted to own you and keep you in a pretty cage, and I wanted to set you free to fly and to love the world. I wanted to be kind and to be wicked, to go and get dirty and smelly with you, and get clean again with you. I wanted you to tame the carnal animal in me by loving what is noble and divine in me. I wanted to fall forever into your eyes and die and be reborn ten thousand times. I wanted to let no mystery of you rest—to turn over every stone in your heart, destroy every protective wall. Not with a flame, with a raging fire—a scorched-earth march to explore you until I found the utter end of you. And then to find that there is no end to you.

  I wanted to just come clean about all that. Do I have any right to say such things to you? I don't know. I surrender. I've never felt anything like this before.

  What do I want now? I said it to you once—to be more like you. I want to be in love with life, and to know the kind of joy I feel from you. I want to know myself and to be who I am deep inside, with no hidden layers. I want to live simply, to have freedom and confidence and to be more friendly. I want to feel as much love for myself as I do for you. I want to determine my own fate—to live every day like it's a new kind of adventure. I want to stumble and fall, and taste the dirt and get up and go looking for more. And I want to know what real love is. No superficial life, no small talk—big talk, deep rivers of thought. I want to know how big a dream I can believe in, to ask what is worth living for and how do I live it?

  I want to hear about your life, and I'd like to be part of it. I like it when you tell me about your friends, your travel plans, your clothes and new shoes, your cat, places you've been and people you've met, music you like, your hometown, your poor little car, your family, favorite movies and iPhone apps, and food you like to eat. I really enjoy hearing about your business and what you hope to do with it, and I love helping if I can.

  I'd like to know where else your mind goes—all the strange places, the thoughts and dreams you rarely share because maybe they're too big or too weird, or just too simple and down-to-earth to seem interesting. I want to know what inspires you, and what shakes you to the core. Can you care more about something that is invisible than about anything else in the world? I'm asking to see what you're made of. What kind of life can you believe in?

I want to be able to sit in comfortable silence with you, just to be simple and sweet and loving with you. I want to be able to talk with you about little things and the biggest stuff there is—how to make miracles out of ordinary thought, how to dream yourself into the most beautiful, unlimited life you can imagine, and to learn to think even greater.

I want to honor you and to learn to love you in absolute freedom, to grow with you in every way one can, and to know what unconditional really means.

I once told you I thought we were becoming close friends, and you tried to set me straight on that—said no, we weren't—said it was not your first rodeo? I wanted to tell you if I had known it was a rodeo, I would have been watching for the bullshit. I bit my tongue instead. It's not your fault, and I've been biting my tongue for too many years. I've just had enough. I've been dying inside for lack of expression. Would you rather I didn't feel this way about you? You might as well ask me to stop breathing. I just don't want to feel bad about it anymore. I am lucky to get to feel this way, lucky to know you and to have spent so much time with you. I wouldn't give up any of it. Would you really want me to take it back—to turn back the clock? Sorry. I love you, I love you, and I can never forget you. You are in me forever. Ride that, cowgirl.

Should I have kept all this to myself? Do you think I'm a bad person? Am I selfish to want you to know my feelings, or would it be stingy of me not to share them? Maybe just watching you walk away would be more loving, but I need to know that I was honest with you. I've had a hard time looking in your eyes lately. It has been eating me up to try to make conversation with you and to not be able to tell you what is in my heart, when all I want to do is scream how much I love you. And I have to know what is possible. I can never live with myself wondering "What if...?"

I'm clearly not able to think objectively about you. I am in my heart, not so much in my head. Have I idealized you too much? My expectations are of myself, to be strong enough to inspire you to love and to dream, as you have done for me. Have I missed something important about you? It may be that I don't really know your temperaments or your changing personality very deeply, don't know all your likes and dislikes, your moods and preferences. Wouldn't it be predictably boring if anyone ever did? Am I seeing something in you—a depth in your character—that isn't really there? Only you can say.

What I know intimately is your spirit, and I cannot exist without it now—it's become part of me. I'll always have it with me, but I am passionately longing to always be able to look in your eyes. That, and to laugh my ass off with you at least once a day.

I've never cared so much about anything in my whole life as I do about you. Knowing you makes me want to be better than I am. Loving you makes me want to be great. Not in a way the world recognizes as great—I don't care what the world thinks, only what you think and what I think. I just mean that I want to live consciously, aware that life is entirely our own creation, and that limits only exist if we believe they are real. I don't want to go back to sleep—it's the same as death to me.

The life I'm inspired to imagine, the one I can care about creating, has you in it. You make me feel this way—no one and nothing else. Do you not know that I would tear my life apart to be with you? Even if I knew it might not last. I don't pretend to know if you and I could be happy together, only that I want very badly to find out. If you wanted it too, I would do anything to be near you—live anywhere, do any work to make a life with you. But if you just don't feel something for me that is deep and meaningful, if there is not enough trust, if you cherish and fear losing your freedom and independence, if you just want something different, I understand.

What I love most about myself is that I can love you this much. I will always be grateful to you for awakening these feelings in me. Maybe it's all too much, yet somehow not nearly enough of the right thing for you. If what I have written does not lighten or open your heart, if it does not feel like a weight removed, then more than anything I want you to just be free of it, whatever it takes. If you can be my friend, but not more, I can find a way to be happy about that. If I have chased you completely away, I hope that at least you will always know that I was sincere with you, that you once inspired someone to dream the grandest things he could imagine, and that he thought enough of you to write them down, from the heart. And I will get to know that, for the first time in my life, I was in love with my whole heart, and I held nothing back.

William

www.roughneckpoet.com

www.ingramcontent.com/pod-product-compliance
Lightning Source LLC
Chambersburg PA
CBHW071656090426
42738CB00009B/1547